To:
Mary Grace & John
Bon Temps Bon Marye

Love,
Monique Boutti Ambra

Recipes from
MULATE'S

From left: Kay Boutté, Murphy Christina, Tiffa Boutté, Kerry Boutté, Monique Boutté Christina, and Renée Christina

Recipes from
MULATE'S

Monique Boutté Christina

Foreword by Angie Delcambre Broussard

Pelican Publishing Company
Gretna 2006

The word "Pelican" and the depiction of a pelican are
trademarks of Pelican Publishing Company, Inc., and are
registered in the U.S. Patent and Trademark Office.

Library of Congress Cataloging-in-Publication Data

Christina, Monique Boutté.
  Recipes from Mulate's / Monique Boutté Christina.
      p. cm.
  Includes index.
  ISBN-13: 978-1-58980-347-3 (hardcover : alk. paper)
  1. Cookery, American—Louisiana style. 2. Cookery, Cajun. I. Mulate's
(Restaurant : New Orleans, La.) II. Title.
  TX715.2.L68C48 2006
  641.59763—dc22
                              2005023150

Photographs and food styling by Paul Rico

Printed in Korea
Published by Pelican Publishing Company, Inc.
1000 Burmaster Street, Gretna, Louisiana 70053

For Renée, my daughter, who amazes and inspires me every day

Monique and Renée

Renée wearing Tiffa's mask from the Krewe of Muses

Contents

Mulate's founder Kerry Boutté and his wife, Tiffa

Foreword

Mulate's is known as the original Cajun restaurant, famous for preserving and celebrating the food, music, and culture found in the small towns and along the bayous of south Louisiana. But the restaurant that prides itself on being true to its roots would never have opened its doors if owner Kerry Boutté hadn't ventured out of Cajun Country and into the restaurants and dance halls of New Orleans, Houston, and even Europe.

Of course, it all started in the small Cajun town of Arnaudville, where Boutté grew up. His mother, Ida, was a renowned Cajun cook. Boutté watched her prepare everything from gumbo and fried chicken to fried calf's brain and corn macque choux. He didn't learn how to cook at her stove, but he learned how to appreciate good cooking. All of the recipes on Mulate's menu find their roots in Ida Boutté's kitchen.

Boutté's own passion for preparing good food started with a job in a meat market in his late teens. Later, he honed his skills working with the Landry family at Don's Restaurant in Morgan City and Houston—ironically, as a manager. In an effort to put out the best product he could, Boutté learned every aspect of the business. He spent time in the kitchen creating his own dishes and learning how to serve delicious, authentic Cajun food night after night. Before long, he knew that having his own restaurant was the only way he could make the decisions and give his customers the meals and the experience he had in mind.

Boutté envisioned offering more than just food based on the Cajun culture he loved. Like most Cajuns growing up in the 1950s, he took his Cajun lifestyle for granted until he spent some time in another part of the world. In the late 1960s, he went into the army and ended up near Frankfurt, Germany. There Boutté developed an interest in art, something he shares with patrons of Mulate's, where works by local artists cover the walls.

Boutté's experience in Germany also introduced him to beer gardens, places where people of all ages came together to eat, drink, and dance to traditional German music. Thousands of miles from home, he immediately saw the connection to his own Cajun culture, where families gathered in their homes to enjoy good food and a unique musical tradition, both passed down from generation to generation. Enjoying the food, music, and culture of the German people, Boutté began to think about creating a similar feeling back home, where the culture was just as fascinating and the food even better.

After a few years in the restaurant business, Boutté was ready to make his vision come to life. In 1980, he opened Mulate's in a small, nondescript building in Breaux Bridge, not far from his hometown. His staff consisted of one cook, two waitresses, and himself—more than enough to serve the two customers who came through the door the first day. The first month saw three thousand dollars in gross sales, but Boutté knew word would spread. He stuck to his goal of serving authentic Cajun food with consistent quality.

Mulate's survived and grew, and after several months Boutté began looking for ways to feature Cajun music in the restaurant. He booked local musician Zachary Richard, and on the first evening Richard played, Boutté knew this was the food, music, and atmosphere he wanted for Mulate's. Only one thing was missing—the customers. That first night, no one came, but Boutté signed Richard up for another night the following week. Eventually, people did come, and Mulate's became known for its Cajun music.

Featuring Cajun musicians at Mulate's not only helped launch a revival of Cajun music. It helped to bring the Cajun culture into the international spotlight. Boutté turned to musicians like Richard and Michael Doucet, who played traditional Cajun music, and to old-timers such as Hector Duhon and Octa Clark. He opened up a space in front of the bandstand and welcomed people to dance. Soon the nights that Mulate's offered live music were the restaurant's hottest nights. Boutté gradually added more musicians until the restaurant had live music seven nights a week.

Even in its first few years, Mulate's attracted people from around the world as well as locals. Visitors and travel writers spread the word about how much fun they had at the little restaurant. With the World's Fair planned for New Orleans in 1984, Boutté saw an opportunity to spread the word even further. He began planning a year in advance, contacting tour-bus operators and bringing them to Mulate's for a taste of what he could provide to their customers. In no time, more than a hundred busses signed up. When the World's Fair came around, not only the tour busses but dozens of other visitors who had read about Mulate's in newspapers and magazines made the trip to Cajun Country to experience it for themselves.

Over the years, Mulate's has attracted more than its fair share of celebrities as well. Musicians ranging from Muddy Waters and Dizzy Gillespie to Huey Lewis and Stevie Ray Vaughan have enjoyed the fun, while a few—most notably Paul Simon and Joe Cocker—have shared the bandstand with local musicians.

Boutté took Mulate's success to Baton Rouge in 1988 and New Orleans in 1990, opening a restaurant in a circa-1885 Italianate warehouse right across the street from the Riverwalk and Convention Center. As Mulate's expanded, Boutté's daughter, Monique, became involved in the family business.

Monique first joined the Mulate's team in 1992 when she needed a part-time job during college. At Mulate's in Baton Rouge, Monique, like her father, learned the business from the inside out by working in every job from hostess and cashier to kitchen and office staff. She married Murphy Christina in 1994 and left the restaurant to devote herself full time to studying accounting. But Mulate's was in her blood and in a few years she talked to Boutté about working in the restaurant again. She couldn't have picked a better time.

Despite Mulate's popularity, the New Orleans restaurant suffered from a period of poor management that left it with significant financial problems. Monique joined the team in May of 1997 and took over management in January of 1998. She straightened out the books and turned the business around. Although Mulate's in Baton Rouge closed in 2001 after losing its lease, the New Orleans location continues to thrive, serving over 250,000 customers each year.

Today Monique and her husband, Murphy, continue to run Mulate's in New Orleans, with Boutté overseeing operations and his wife, Tiffa, contributing to public relations. What Boutté appreciates most about Monique's involvement is that she shares his commitment to maintaining the quality of the food and music—the experience—that Mulate's offers. Boutté is proud to have passed on to his daughter a devotion to the culture they both love.

Angie Delcambre Broussard

Acknowledgments

Thanks

First, I'd like to thank my mom, Kay Boutté, for her contributions, her patience in perfecting recipes, and all of her hard work.

Thank you to my dad, Kerry Boutté, for all of the opportunities he has given me.

And to my husband, Murphy Christina, for keeping me laughing.

Thanks very much to:

My family members who contributed recipes to the cookbook.

Our customers—many of whom inspired me to write this cookbook.

The management and staff at Mulate's of New Orleans—you make it happen every day!

Perry Watts for his help with recipes and for keeping our food both delicious and consistent.

About the contributors:

My grandmother, Ida Boutté, was a great cook and inspiration to me. We would go to her house on Sundays for lunch. I'll always remember eating fresh tomatoes with salt, pepper, and a little mayonnaise—so simple and delicious. She passed away suddenly in April of 1997.

Joyce Kolb was my aunt and a dear sister to my father. She was also a terrific cook. She cooked an unbelievable Thanksgiving feast every year. I was really excited to get some of her recipes for the book back in 2001. She passed away suddenly in June of 2002.

Tiffa Boutté is my father's wife. She taught me how to make a delicious homemade corn macque choux. Then, she improved an already terrific recipe by adding crawfish tails to it. You must try this recipe—it's absolutely awesome!

Gab Robin is my mom's brother. He and his wife, Mary, always put together fabulous holiday meals. Gab has been a butcher since the 1970s. He blends his own seasonings and is known for his specialty meats like stuffed brisket, boudin, smoked sausage, and stuffed pork chops. I continue to be inspired each time I eat a meal at his house.

Mark Robin is also my mom's brother. He doesn't cook too often, but the recipe I've included is a staple in his household.

Goldie Comeaux is my father's ex-wife, who owns and operates Mulate's in Breaux Bridge, Louisiana. She remains a good friend of mine whom I respect very much. She has her own cookbook that showcases many of her delicious recipes.

Introduction

I have been in the restaurant business since 1992, and I have worked almost every position from hostess to fry cook to floor manager to office manager. My favorite place has always been in the kitchen. It is the heart of the restaurant. I love to cook, and—luckily—it's something that I'm pretty good at doing.

I learned to cook by observing my family—my parents, grandparents, aunts, and uncles. Almost everyone in my family is a great cook. My dad is an amazing cook. He *never* cooks with a recipe, and he has cooked some of the best meals of my life. His recipes don't require a lot of ingredients. He keeps it simple. Everything he cooks, he cooks perfectly—no frills, just wonderful and delicious. I don't think he knows how truly talented he is.

All you need to cook a good meal is a little skill and lots of patience. Anyone can pick up a few cooking skills these days by watching cooking shows on TV. Finding the patience and the time is the hard part!

Cooking isn't just about the recipe. Recipes are only guidelines for cooking a good meal. True cooking is about putting your heart and soul into the dish. My greatest achievement in the kitchen is seeing people smile when they eat the dish I've prepared. I love cooking for friends and family. Having people over, laughing and talking in the kitchen, enjoying a meal— these are the things that make life worth living.

Through this cookbook, I want to share that feeling with you. With these guidelines—and your heart and soul—you'll experience the success of making people smile with your creations. I hope you enjoy this cookbook as much as I've enjoyed putting it together!

Appetizers

Dancing at Mulate's

Best Stuffed Mushrooms!
ALEXANDRIA, LOUISIANA

The blackened alligator was excellent!
LAS VEGAS, NEVADA

Excellent gator!
BEACHWOOD, OHIO

Wonderful Food, Great Music & Dancing!
JEFFERSONVILLE, INDIANA

We come to N.O. every year & we have to come here 3 or 4 times in a weekend before we leave. The best in the world!
SAFETY HARBOR, FLORIDA

Bite-Size Catfish

12 catfish filets, 2-3 oz. each
3 cups cornmeal
2-3 tsp. salt
1 tsp. cayenne pepper
2-3 cups oil for frying

Rinse and dry catfish. Cut into bite-size pieces. Place cornmeal in a 9x13 pan. Season cornmeal with salt and cayenne to your taste, mixing well. Put catfish bites in seasoned cornmeal, coating well. Fry in oil at 375 degrees for 6-7 minutes. Serve with Tartar or Cocktail Sauce (see index for both). Serves 4-6.

Fried Alligator

2 lb. alligator loin meat
3 cups flour
2-3 tsp. salt
1 tsp. cayenne pepper
1 cup milk
2 eggs, beaten
2-3 cups oil for frying

Rinse and dry alligator. Tenderize using a "hammer-style" tenderizing tool. Cut into bite-size pieces. Place flour in a 9x13 pan. Add salt and cayenne to your taste, mixing well. In a shallow bowl, mix milk and eggs. Dip alligator bites in egg wash, then place in flour mixture, coating well. Fry in oil at 375 degrees for 4-5 minutes. This is delicious with Remoulade Dressing (see index) as a dipping sauce. Serves 4-6.

Grilled Alligator

Blackened Alligator

2 lb. alligator loin meat
1 tbsp. Mulate's Cajun Seasoning
2 tbsp. Mulate's Blackening Seasoning
2 tbsp. oil

Rinse and dry alligator. Tenderize using a "hammer-style" tenderizing tool. Cut into bite-size pieces. Season meat with Cajun seasoning, then with blackening seasoning. Heat oil in a large nonstick skillet. Cook alligator over medium-high heat, stirring frequently, for about 3-5 minutes. This is delicious with Remoulade Dressing (see index) as a dipping sauce. If you want less spice, omit blackening seasoning and you'll have simple and tasty Grilled Alligator. Serves 4-6.

Hot Crabmeat Dip

$^1/_2$ stick butter
2 stalks celery, diced
2 cloves garlic, diced
8 oz. cream cheese
8 oz. processed cheese
1 tbsp. milk
1 tsp. cayenne pepper
$^1/_2$ tsp. black pepper
1 bunch green onions, chopped
1 lb. lump or jumbo lump crabmeat, picked over for shells

In medium saucepan, melt butter and add celery and garlic. Cook over medium heat for about 15 minutes. Add cream cheese and processed cheese—lower heat, and stir constantly until melted. Add milk and mix well. Add peppers and green onions, blending well. Fold in crabmeat. Serve warm on crackers or toast points.

My grandparents, Raoul Joseph Boutté and Ida Colon Boutté

Ida's Crabmeat Mornay

$1/2$ stick butter
1 small bunch green onions, chopped
2 tbsp. flour
1 tsp. salt
1 tsp. cayenne pepper
$1/2$ tsp. black pepper
$1/2$ pt. heavy cream
$1/2$ pt. half-and-half
$1/2$ lb. Swiss cheese, grated
1 lb. lump crabmeat

Melt butter and add green onions. Sauté over medium heat for 10 minutes. Blend in flour, then add seasonings. Add cream, half-and-half, and cheese. Stir constantly until cheese is melted. Fold in crabmeat and continue cooking just long enough for crabmeat to get hot. Serve as a hot dip with Melba toast or in patty shells.

Ida Colon Boutté
Arnaudville, LA

Marinated Crab Claws

5 tbsp. extra-virgin olive oil
$1/4$ cup water
5 dashes hot sauce
2 cloves garlic, crushed
3 tbsp. Worcestershire sauce
1 tbsp. white vinegar
2 tsp. black pepper
1 tsp. salt
Juice of 2 lemons
1 lb. fresh crab claws

Mix all ingredients except crab. Add crab claws, and stir until all are coated. Place in refrigerator for at least 3 hours, stirring every 30 minutes or so. Serves 4.

Sautéed Crab Claws

1 stick butter
3 cloves garlic, minced
1 tbsp. Worcestershire sauce
1 tsp. Mulate's Cajun Seasoning
$1/4$ tsp. cayenne pepper
1 lb. fresh crab claws
1 tbsp. chopped parsley

In a large sauté pan, melt butter over medium-high heat. Add garlic and cook for 3 minutes, stirring frequently to prevent garlic from browning. Stir in Worcestershire sauce, Cajun seasoning, and cayenne. Add crab claws and stir to coat in the sauce. Cook for about 5 minutes. Sprinkle in parsley and remove from heat. Serves 4.

Shrimp and Oysters en Brochette

2 tbsp. butter
3 cloves garlic, minced
1 tbsp. Mulate's Cajun Seasoning
$\frac{1}{2}$ lb. medium shrimp (40/50 count)
1 pt. oysters (about 20 oysters)
20 slices center-cut bacon
20 toothpicks
2 cups oil for frying

In a sauté pan, melt butter over medium-high heat. Add garlic and half of Cajun seasoning. Sauté, stirring constantly, for about 3 minutes. Add shrimp and cook for about 5 minutes. Remove shrimp from pan and set aside to cool. Add oysters and other half of Cajun seasoning to pan and sauté for 3 minutes. Remove oysters from pan and set aside to cool. Wrap 1 shrimp and 1 oyster in 1 bacon slice. Hold closed with 1 toothpick. Continue this procedure for all 20 brochettes.

In a heavy pot, heat oil to about 350 degrees. Place brochettes in oil and cook for about 5-7 minutes, or until bacon is cooked through. You will have to work in batches—maybe 2 or 3 batches for all 20 brochettes. Serve with Tartar Sauce and Remoulade Dressing (see index for both) for dipping. Serves 6-8 as an appetizer.

Shrimp Supreme

$1/2$ stick butter
1 small onion, diced
3 cloves garlic, diced
2 tbsp. flour
1 cup heavy cream
1 cup half-and-half
1 lb. medium shrimp, boiled and coarsely chopped
1 tsp. Mulate's Cajun Seasoning
$1/4$ cup chopped green onions
1 cup shredded Monterey Jack cheese
6 puff pastry shells, baked

In a large saucepan, melt butter over medium heat. Add onion and garlic, stirring frequently. Be sure not to brown the garlic. Cook for 10 minutes. Add flour and stir constantly until well blended. Add cream and stir until blended. Add half-and-half and stir until blended. Bring to a boil, reduce heat, and simmer for 5 minutes. Add shrimp and seasoning; cook for 10 minutes, stirring frequently. Add green onions and cheese; cook for 2-3 minutes. Spoon into puff pastry shells and serve. Serves 6.

Spicy Shrimp Dip

6-8 cups water
2 tbsp. Mulate's Cajun Seasoning
1 lb. medium shrimp, peeled

In a large saucepot, boil water and seasoning. Add shrimp, and when water begins to boil again, turn heat off. Let shrimp soak for 10 minutes, then drain and coarsely chop.

Dip

$^1/_2$ cup mayonnaise
1 tsp. Mulate's Cajun Seasoning
1 tsp. onion powder
$^1/_2$ tsp. garlic powder
1 tsp. Worcestershire sauce
1 tsp. hot sauce
8 oz. cream cheese, softened
$^1/_4$ cup thinly sliced green onions

In a mixing bowl, blend mayonnaise, Cajun seasoning, onion powder, garlic powder, Worcestershire sauce, and hot sauce. Add cream cheese and green onions, mixing until smooth. Add chopped shrimp and mix well. Chill for at least 30 minutes. Serve on crackers or Melba toast.

Stuffed Mushrooms

Mulate's Crabmeat Stuffing (see index)
30 medium mushroom caps

Place approximately 1 oz. stuffing in each mushroom cap.

To Bake: Place stuffed mushrooms on a baking sheet. Sprinkle with Parmesan cheese, if desired. Bake at 375 degrees for 15-20 minutes.

To Fry: Combine 2 beaten eggs and 1 cup milk. Dip stuffed mushrooms into egg wash and then dredge in 3 cups breadcrumbs, coating well. Fry in 2-3 cups oil at approximately 350 degrees until golden brown. Serve with Tartar Sauce (see index).

Sweet-Hot Deviled Eggs

6 hardboiled eggs
$^1/_3$ cup mayonnaise
1 tbsp. yellow mustard
$^1/_2$ tbsp. sweet pickle relish
$^1/_4$ tsp. cayenne pepper
Paprika for garnish

Split eggs in half and place yolks in a medium bowl and white halves on a plate. Add remaining ingredients (except paprika) to yolks, mixing until well blended and smooth. Fill the whites with this mixture. Sprinkle with paprika. Makes 12.

Salads

This is the best yet!
PUNXSUTAWNEY, PENNSYLVANIA

Excellent food & great service!
KEITHVILLE, LOUISIANA

All right baby!
ROME, ITALY

Loved the dance floor & band! This is a great place to bring kids!
KINGWOOD, TEXAS

Had such fun last night—came back for lunch!
FOREST LAKE, MINNESOTA

Arugula Salad with Fig-Infused Vinaigrette

5 cups fresh arugula
$1/4$ cup pine nuts
1 small can mandarin slices, drained
$1/2$ small red onion, thinly sliced

Wash and dry arugula and place in a large serving bowl. Toast pine nuts in a small nonstick pan over medium heat. Remove from heat when golden brown and add to arugula. Add mandarin slices and onion.

Fig-Infused Vinaigrette

$3/4$ cup extra-virgin olive oil
$1/4$ cup fig-infused balsamic vinegar
$1/4$ tsp. Dijon mustard
1 tsp. salt
3 turns fresh-cracked black pepper

In a small bowl, whisk olive oil, vinegar, and mustard until smooth. Blend in salt and pepper and pour over salad. Toss and enjoy!

Tiffa Boutté
New Orleans, LA

Cole Slaw

1 medium head cabbage
1 tsp. sugar
1 tsp. black pepper
$^1/_2$ tsp. salt
$^3/_4$ cup mayonnaise

Cut cabbage head in half. Shred cabbage or cut cabbage into small, thin slices. Place in large mixing bowl. In a small bowl, mix remaining ingredients until smooth and creamy. Pour dressing onto cabbage and mix well. Serve immediately or let soften slightly in refrigerator. Serves 8-10.

Macaroni Salad

4 cups uncooked small elbow macaroni
4 hardboiled eggs
4 sweet gherkins
3 carrots
4 stalks celery
1 medium onion
2 cups mayonnaise
$^1/_3$ cup white vinegar
4 tbsp. sugar
$^1/_2$ tsp. salt
1 tsp. black pepper
$^1/_2$ tsp. cayenne pepper

Boil macaroni and drain. Grate eggs, gherkins, carrots, celery, and onion, using the largest holes on your grater. In a large bowl, mix cooked macaroni and grated vegetables. Stir in mayonnaise. In a separate bowl, mix vinegar and sugar until sugar has dissolved. Add dry seasonings and pour over salad, mixing well. Cover and chill for at least 24 hours. This recipe is great for parties and bar-b-ques.

Joyce Boutté Kolb
Arnaudville, LA

Lump Crabmeat Salad

1 cup mayonnaise
$^{1}/_{4}$ cup Creole mustard
3 dashes hot sauce
$^{1}/_{4}$ tsp. garlic powder
$^{1}/_{4}$ cup finely sliced green onions
1 lb. lump crabmeat, picked over for shells
1 head lettuce, chopped

In a mixing bowl, combine all ingredients except crabmeat and lettuce. Blend well. Fold in crabmeat. Place salad mixture on top of chopped lettuce. Serves 4.

Potato Salad

3 large potatoes
$1^{1}/_{2}$ tsp. salt
$^{1}/_{2}$ tsp. black pepper
$^{1}/_{2}$ tsp. cayenne pepper
4 large hardboiled eggs
4 tbsp. mayonnaise
1 tbsp. + 1 tsp. mustard
1 tsp. vinegar
25 small green olives stuffed with pimentos, sliced

Remove skin from potatoes and cut potatoes into 1-inch pieces. Boil until tender, then drain. Put cooked potatoes into a large mixing bowl, sprinkle with dry seasonings, and mix well. Cut the eggs in half. Place yolks in small bowl, and cut whites into the seasoned potato mixture. Mash yolks with the back of a fork and add mayonnaise, mustard, vinegar, and olive slices. Mix until smooth, then add to potato mixture and mix until texture is to your liking. You can spice up potato salad with minced celery, thinly sliced green onions, minced shallots—just throw in a little of whatever you like!

Variation: In place of the olives, use 1-2 tbsp. sweet pickle relish.

Shrimp Remoulade

10 cups water
2 tbsp. Mulate's Cajun Seasoning
2 lb. medium shrimp, peeled
1 head lettuce, chopped
Remoulade Dressing (see index)

In a large stockpot, boil water and add seasoning and shrimp. Bring water back to a boil and cook shrimp for 5 minutes. Drain shrimp and let cool. Place 6-8 shrimp on a bed of lettuce on each plate. Top with Remoulade Dressing. Serves 10.

Shrimp Salad

8 cups water
2 tbsp. Mulate's Cajun Seasoning
$1^1/_2$ lb. medium shrimp, peeled
1 stalk celery, diced
2 hardboiled eggs
4 tbsp. mayonnaise
$^1/_2$ tbsp. Creole mustard
$^1/_4$ tsp. cayenne pepper

In a large stockpot, boil water and add seasoning and shrimp. Bring water back to a boil and cook shrimp for 5 minutes. Drain shrimp, let cool, and coarsely chop.

In a medium bowl, mix shrimp and celery. Remove yolks from eggs and set aside. Chop egg whites and mix into shrimp mixture. In a separate small bowl, mash egg yolks and add mayonnaise, Creole mustard, and cayenne, mixing well. When the "dressing" is well blended and smooth, pour it into the shrimp mix. Stir until dressing is spread evenly throughout. Serve on lettuce or on toasted bread.

Gumbos
and Soups

Kerry and Monique in the kitchen together

Great! . . . As usual. The alligator and gumbo were to die for!
Keep up the good work!
COFFEEVILLE, MISSISSIPPI

Excellent Gumbo!
CLOUTIERVILLE, LOUISIANA

Good music & Gumbo!
MEMPHIS, TENNESSEE

Absolutely Awesome!
HOUMA, LOUISIANA

Great Gumbo!
ABBOTSFORD, BRITISH COLUMBIA, CANADA

Baked Potato Soup

4 large baking potatoes
6 tbsp. butter
$1/3$ cup flour
10 cups whole milk
1 tbsp. Mulate's Cajun Seasoning
$1/2$ tsp. salt
$1/8$ tsp. cayenne pepper
$1/2$ cup chopped green onions
2 cups shredded cheddar cheese
8 slices crisp-cooked bacon
4 oz. sour cream

Preheat oven to 400 degrees. Rinse and dry potatoes. Wrap potatoes individually in aluminum foil. Bake for 1 hour 15 minutes. Remove from oven, unwrap, and slice in half. Scoop potatoes out of the skins into a medium bowl, discarding skins.

In a large soup pot, melt butter over medium-low heat. Add flour, stirring constantly with a whisk. Once flour is dissolved, cook for about 3 minutes, stirring constantly. Raise heat to medium; add milk, 2 cups at a time, still stirring constantly. Cook for about 15 minutes, until thick. Reduce heat to medium low and add potatoes, dry seasonings, 2 tbsp. green onions, and $1\frac{1}{2}$ cups shredded cheddar cheese. Crumble bacon and add to soup, reserving 1 tbsp. Mix until well blended. Stir in sour cream. Serve using remaining green onions, cheese, and bacon as a garnish. Serves 8 as an appetizer.

Chicken Noodle Soup

3 chicken breast halves, bone in, skin on
1 tbsp. olive oil
1 tbsp. Mulate's Cajun Seasoning
2 qt. low-sodium chicken broth
2 stalks celery, sliced
3 carrots, sliced
8 oz. pasta of choice (I prefer wide egg noodles or penne)
Fresh-cracked black pepper

Preheat the oven to 350 degrees. Place the chicken breasts on a sheet pan and rub with olive oil. Sprinkle seasoning on the breasts. Bake for 40 minutes or until cooked through. Remove the breasts from the oven and let them cool enough to handle. Discard the skin, remove the meat from the bones, and dice the chicken.

In a large, heavy pot, bring the chicken broth to a boil, and then reduce the heat to a simmer. Stir in the celery, carrots, and pasta. Add a little (about 3 turns) fresh-cracked black pepper. Simmer for about 10-15 minutes, or until pasta is cooked. Add the chicken and heat through. Serves 6.

Chicken and Sausage Gumbo

1 large onion, diced
1 small bell pepper, diced
1 tbsp. oil
1 tbsp. salt
1 tsp. cayenne pepper
4 qt. water
1 cup dark roux
3 lb. chicken, cut up
3 links smoked sausage, cut into $^{1}/_{2}$-inch pieces
3 cups cooked white rice

In a large pot, sauté onion and bell pepper in oil for about 10 minutes. Add seasonings, then water, and bring to a boil. Add roux and stir constantly until melted. Add chicken and let simmer on medium-high heat for 1 hour. Add smoked sausage and let cook for 20 minutes more. Turn the heat off and let the gumbo rest for 20-30 minutes before serving. Serve over white rice. Serves 6-8.

You'll notice that I don't make my own roux. I use roux in a jar that you can find on the seasonings aisle in your local grocery store. Although many people will say that making your own roux for gumbo makes a difference, I simply don't think it does. The jarred roux is consistent and always makes delicious gumbos and stews. Making your own roux also requires time, which we all don't have a lot of. So, don't worry, you can still make an authentic, delicious gumbo with jarred roux.

I also like to let my gumbo "rest" before serving. I find that the flavors come together and it makes the gumbo even better. Use the 30 minutes to make your potato salad, and then enjoy an old Cajun favorite combo!

Crab and Corn Bisque

1 stick butter
2 medium onions, diced
3 cloves garlic, diced
$^1/_2$ cup flour
1 tbsp. salt
1 tsp. black pepper
1 tsp. cayenne pepper
1 qt. half-and-half
6 cups whole milk
1 can whole-kernel corn
1 can cream-style corn
1 lb. lump crabmeat, picked over for shells
1 lb. claw crabmeat, picked over for shells

In a large soup pot, melt butter and add onions. Sauté onions for 10 minutes. Add garlic and sauté for 5 minutes. Stir frequently and make sure garlic doesn't brown. Over medium-low heat, add flour a little at a time, stirring constantly. A paste will form. Add seasonings and continue stirring. Gradually add half-and-half and milk, then raise heat to medium high. Stir constantly until well blended. Bring just to a boil, then reduce heat to medium low. Add both cans of corn and the crabmeat and partially cover. Continue cooking, stirring frequently, until soup is desired thickness, about 15 minutes. Taste soup and season to your preference, if necessary. Serves 8 as an appetizer.

Duck and Andouille Gumbo

1 duck, 5-5$^{1}/_{2}$ lb.
2 medium onions, diced
1 small bell pepper, diced
3 stalks celery, diced
3 cloves garlic, minced
1 tbsp. oil
4 cups reserved duck stock
3 qt. water
$^{3}/_{4}$ cup dark roux
1 tbsp. salt
1 tsp. cayenne pepper
1 lb. andouille, sliced

Place duck in a large stockpot and cover with some water. Boil duck for 1 hour, and then remove and let it cool enough to handle. Reserve 4 cups duck stock—be sure to skim the grease off of the stock. Remove the skin from the duck, debone, and cube the meat.

Meanwhile, in another large stockpot, sauté vegetables in oil until transparent, about 15-20 minutes. Add duck stock and water and bring to a boil. Add roux, stirring constantly until melted. Add seasonings, duck, and sliced andouille. Let simmer for 45 minutes. Turn the heat off and let the gumbo rest for 20-30 minutes before serving. Serves 8-10.

Seafood Gumbo

4 qt. water
3 lb. medium shrimp, shells on
2 medium onions, diced
1 small bell pepper, diced
1 cup dark roux
2 lb. claw crabmeat
12-24 oysters
1 tbsp. salt
1 tsp. cayenne pepper
4 cups cooked white rice

In a large pot, bring water to a boil. Boil shrimp for 10 minutes. Let stand 3 minutes. Remove shrimp from stock with a strainer. Peel shrimp and discard the shells. Add onions and bell pepper to stock. Bring back to a boil. Add roux, stirring constantly until melted. Let boil for 30 minutes. Add shrimp, crabmeat, oysters, and seasonings. Let simmer for 5 minutes more. Turn the heat off and let the gumbo rest for 20-30 minutes. Serve over white rice. Serves 8-10.

Shrimp and Okra Gumbo

1 tbsp. oil
2 medium onions, diced
1 small bell pepper, diced
3 cloves garlic, chopped
2 lb. cut okra, fresh or frozen
1 tbsp. salt
$1^1/_2$ tsp. cayenne pepper
9 cups water
$^1/_4$ cup dark roux
$1^1/_2$ lb. medium shrimp, peeled and deveined
3 cups cooked white rice

In a large pot, heat oil and add onions, bell pepper, garlic, and okra. Cook over medium heat for 30-40 minutes, stirring frequently. The okra will be slimy at first, but once you cook it for a while, the slime will disappear. Add seasonings and stir. Add water, stir, and bring to a boil. Add roux, stir frequently, and make sure that roux dissolves completely. Boil for about 15 minutes. Add shrimp, and bring back to a boil. Turn off the heat and let the gumbo rest for 20-30 minutes. Serve over white rice. Serves 6-8.

Zydeco Gumbo

2 medium onions, diced
1 medium bell pepper, diced
3 stalks celery, diced
5 cloves garlic, diced
3 pkg. frozen cut okra, 10 oz. each
1 tbsp. oil
1 tbsp. Mulate's Cajun Seasoning
$\frac{1}{2}$ tsp. cayenne pepper
$\frac{1}{2}$ tsp. black pepper
4 qt. water
1 cup roux
1 lb. 50/60 count shrimp, peeled
2 lb. boneless, skinless chicken thighs, trimmed and cut into smaller pieces
1 lb. smoked sausage, sliced $\frac{1}{4}$ inch thick
3 cups cooked white rice

In a large soup pot, sauté onions, bell pepper, celery, garlic, and okra in oil for about 20-30 minutes. Add seasonings and stir until blended. Add water and bring to a boil. Add roux and stir until dissolved. Add shrimp and chicken pieces; bring back to a boil. Continue to boil for approximately 40 minutes. Add smoked sausage; boil for 10 minutes. Turn off the heat and let the gumbo rest for 30-45 minutes. Serve over white rice. Serves 6-8. This is a customer favorite!

Entrées

Mulate's seafood platter, featuring Fried Crawfish, Fried Catfish, Stuffed Crab, Fried Shrimp, Sautéed Haricots Verts, Fried Oysters, Mulate's Chicken and Sausage Jambalaya, and Crawfish Etouffée on the side.

*I have to say it was great! I felt like I was in Breaux Bridge,
Louisiana—Excellent!*
ARNAUDVILLE, LOUISIANA

Catfish was awesome!
CHICAGO, ILLINOIS

Great Red Beans & Rice!
CORPUS CHRISTI, TEXAS

Love that Jambalaya!
SAN JOSE, CALIFORNIA

*Mulate's food is the big reason I wanted to come to N'awlins.
Cajun cookin' at its best! Came here twice during our short stay!
Highly recommended!*
WINNIPEG, MANITOBA, CANADA

Baked Chicken

1 large onion, minced
1 medium bell pepper, minced
3 cloves garlic, minced
1$\frac{1}{2}$ tsp. salt
1$\frac{1}{2}$ tsp. cayenne pepper
4-5 lb. chicken
2 tbsp. Mulate's Cajun Seasoning
1 tbsp. oil
$\frac{1}{2}$ cup water
1 medium onion, cut into 8 wedges

Preheat oven to 375 degrees. In a small bowl, combine the minced onion, bell pepper, and garlic, and mix well. Add salt and cayenne, mixing well.

Season the inside and outside of chicken with Cajun seasoning. Cut 2-3 slits in each side of the breast, thighs, and legs. Stuff the slits with the onion mixture. Place any excess in the cavity of the chicken.

Lightly grease a roasting pot with the oil and add the water. Place chicken in pot and place onion wedges around chicken. Cover and bake for 1 hour. Turn oven up to 400 degrees, uncover chicken, and bake for 15 minutes more. Serves 4.

Chicken Stew

3 lb. chicken, cut up
1$^1/_2$ tbsp. Mulate's Cajun Seasoning
1 tbsp. oil
1 large onion, diced
1 medium bell pepper, diced
4 cups water
1 tsp. salt
$^1/_4$ cup roux
3 cups cooked white rice

Season chicken with the Cajun seasoning. Heat oil in a large saucepot over medium heat. Brown chicken on all sides, then remove from pot. Add onion and bell pepper to pot, and sauté for about 5 minutes. Add water and make sure that all drippings are scraped from the pot and combined with the water. Add salt, and bring to a boil. Add roux and stir frequently until dissolved. Put chicken back in pot. Reduce heat to medium low, and simmer, partially covered, for 40 minutes. Remove cover and simmer for 20 minutes more. Serve over rice. Serves 4-6.

Fried Chicken

8 eggs
1 cup light beer
2 tbsp. Mulate's Cajun Seasoning
2 tsp. cayenne pepper
$1/2$ tsp. baking powder
4-5 lb. chicken, cut up
3-4 cups flour
3 cups oil for frying

In a large bowl, mix eggs, beer, Cajun seasoning, cayenne, and baking powder. Rinse and dry chicken. Place chicken in marinade. Place bowl in refrigerator and marinate overnight.

Place chicken in flour, and coat well. Fry in oil at 350 degrees for approximately 15 minutes.

Fried Shrimp

$1^1/_2$ lb. 26/30 count shrimp
3 cups flour
2-3 tsp. salt
1 tsp. cayenne pepper
1 cup milk
2 eggs, beaten
2-3 cups oil for frying

Remove all peeling from shrimp, except the tails. Devein shrimp. Rinse and dry shrimp. Place flour in a 9x13 pan. Add salt and cayenne to your taste, and mix well. In a shallow bowl, mix milk and eggs. Dip shrimp in egg wash, then place in flour mixture, coating well. Fry in oil at 375 degrees for 5-6 minutes. Serve with Tartar or Cocktail sauces (see index for both). Serves 4.

Shrimp are sized according to how many will come to a pound. For example, 16 to 20 shrimp will come to a pound of 16/20 count. Just remember, the lower the number in the count, the larger the shrimp. Another example is that 40 to 50 shrimp will come to a pound of 40/50 count. These shrimp would be considerably smaller than the 16/20s we use in this recipe.

Barbecued Shrimp

3 sticks butter
$^1/_4$ cup chopped garlic
2 tsp. Mulate's Cajun Seasoning
2 lb. 16/20 count shrimp, shells on
$^1/_3$ cup Italian breadcrumbs
1 loaf French bread, warmed

Melt butter over medium heat in a large saucepan. Add garlic and season-ing, and stir frequently to make sure garlic doesn't brown. Cook for 5

Kerry cooks one of his specialties—Barbecued Shrimp

minutes. Add shrimp, and cook for about 2 minutes on each side. Add breadcrumbs and mix well. Immediately serve shrimp in a bowl with plenty of sauce. Peel and eat shrimp, and use French bread to "sop up" the sauce! Serves 4.

Kerry Boutté
Owner, Mulate's of New Orleans

Shrimp Creole

4 tbsp. butter
1 medium onion, diced
1 small bell pepper, diced
3 cloves garlic, chopped
$1^1/_2$ cups water
8-oz. can tomato sauce
$^1/_2$ tsp. thyme
$^1/_2$ tsp. dried sweet basil
1 tsp. salt
$^1/_2$ tsp. cayenne pepper
1 lb. medium shrimp, peeled and deveined
2 cups cooked white rice

In a medium saucepot, melt the butter and sauté onion, bell pepper, and garlic for about 10 minutes. Stir in water, tomato sauce, and dry seasonings. Cover and simmer for 30 minutes, stirring occasionally. Add shrimp, cover, and simmer for 20 minutes, stirring occasionally. Serve over rice. Serves 4.

Shrimp Stew

2 medium onions, diced
1 small bell pepper, diced
3 cloves garlic, chopped
1 tbsp. oil
2$\frac{1}{2}$ cups water or shrimp stock
$\frac{1}{2}$ cup roux
1$\frac{1}{2}$ lb. medium shrimp, peeled and deveined
1 tsp. salt
$\frac{1}{2}$ tsp. cayenne pepper
$\frac{1}{4}$ cup chopped green onions
2 cups cooked white rice

In a medium saucepot, sauté onions, bell pepper, and garlic in oil for about 10 minutes. Add water and roux. Stir until roux dissolves completely. Simmer on medium heat for 10 minutes. Reduce heat to medium low, add shrimp and seasonings, and cover. Simmer for 20 minutes, stirring occasionally. Add green onions and serve over rice. Serves 4.

Stuffed Shrimp

1 stick butter
1 medium onion, diced
1 small bell pepper, diced
3 stalks celery, diced
3 cloves garlic, chopped
1 tsp. Mulate's Cajun Seasoning
$^1/_4$ tsp. thyme
$^1/_4$ cup water
$^1/_2$ lb. medium shrimp, coarsely chopped
$^1/_2$ lb. claw or lump crabmeat
$^3/_4$ cup breadcrumbs

Melt butter over medium-low heat. Add vegetables and cook for 25 minutes, stirring occasionally. Add dry seasonings, water, shrimp, and crabmeat and simmer for 8 minutes. Turn off heat, add bread crumbs, and mix well.

Shrimp

1 lb. 16/20 count shrimp
1 tsp. Mulate's Cajun Seasoning
$^1/_2$ stick butter, melted

Preheat oven to 450 degrees. Peel shrimp and leave the tail on. Devein shrimp, and split well down the center. Be sure not to cut shrimp in half. Sprinkle shrimp with Cajun seasoning. Mold stuffing along the center of the split shrimp. Place shrimp in pan, pour melted butter over shrimp, cover, and bake for 15 minutes. Uncover, sprinkle with Parmesan cheese, if desired, and bake for 2 minutes more. Serves 4.

Boiled Shrimp and Crawfish

Boiled Shrimp

8 cups water
2 tbsp. Mulate's Cajun Seasoning
1 lb. shrimp, any size, shells on

Bring water and seasoning to a boil. Add shrimp and bring back to a boil. Turn heat off, cover, and let shrimp soak for 20 minutes. Drain shrimp and serve with Cocktail Sauce (see index). Serves 2-4.

Boiled Crawfish

9 gal. water
5 lemons, quartered
13 cups crab boil*
4 cups cayenne pepper
8 onions, quartered
3 heads garlic
2 oranges, quartered
3 lb. small red potatoes
1 sack crawfish, about 40 lb.
8-12 ears corn

In an extra-large stockpot, bring all of the ingredients except the crawfish and corn to a boil. Add crawfish and bring back to a boil. When water begins to boil again, turn off heat and add corn. Let crawfish and seasonings soak for 20 minutes. Try to cool off the pot as soon as possible. We usually hose down the outside of the pot, which works really well. After 20 minutes of soaking and cooling, drain the crawfish and seasonings. Serves 8.

Serving Suggestion: Cover a long table with one layer of garbage bags and a few layers of newspaper. Pour crawfish over the center of the table and dig in!

*You can usually find crab boil in the seasonings section of your grocery store. If the crab boil you use *does not* have salt in it, add 6 cups salt.

Crawfish Etouffée

$^1/_2$ stick butter
1 medium onion, diced
1 small bell pepper, diced
1 tsp. salt
1 tsp. cayenne pepper
2 tsp. flour
$^1/_2$ cup water
1 lb. peeled crawfish tails
$^1/_4$ cup chopped green onions
2 cups cooked white rice

In a large saucepan, melt butter over medium heat. Add onion and bell pepper, and cook until transparent and tender—about 15 minutes. Add seasonings, then flour, stirring constantly. Add water; mix well. Add crawfish and simmer for 10 minutes. Add green onions and simmer for 3 minutes more. Serve over rice. Serves 4.

Fried Crawfish

2 lb. peeled crawfish tails
3 cups flour
2-3 tsp. salt
1 tsp. cayenne pepper
1 cup milk
2 eggs, beaten
2-3 cups oil for frying

Rinse and dry crawfish. Place flour in a 9x13 pan. Add salt and cayenne to your taste, and mix well. In a shallow bowl, mix milk and eggs. Dip crawfish in egg wash, then place in flour mixture, coating well. Fry in oil at 375 degrees for 4-5 minutes. Serve with Cocktail Sauce (see index). Serves 4-6.

Preparing the corn to make macque choux

Crawfish Macque Choux

9 ears corn
$^1/_4$ cup oil
1 onion, chopped
$^1/_2$ small bell pepper, chopped
1 tsp. salt
$^1/_2$ tsp. black pepper
$^1/_4$ tsp. cayenne pepper
1 lb. peeled crawfish tails, coarsely chopped

Using a knife, cut the corn off the cobs. Then, using the blunt edge of the knife, scrape the cobs to get all of the juices. Heat oil in large saucepot. Cook corn on medium heat for 10 minutes. Add onion, bell pepper, and seasonings. Cook on medium for 40 minutes, stirring frequently. Add crawfish tails, stir, and heat through. Serves 4-6.

Tiffa Boutté
New Orleans, LA

Crawfish Pasta

2 sticks butter
1 medium onion, diced
1 small bell pepper, diced
2 cans cream of mushroom soup
2 lb. peeled crawfish tails, with fat
$\frac{1}{2}$ tsp. cayenne pepper
$\frac{1}{2}$ tsp. black pepper
1 pt. half-and-half
1 tsp. flour
1 lb. processed cheese
1 lb. your favorite pasta

In large saucepot, melt 1 stick butter and sauté onion and bell pepper. When vegetables are transparent, add soup. Cook on medium heat for 10 minutes. Add crawfish and seasonings and cook for another 10 minutes. Add a little half-and-half as needed to prevent sticking.

In a separate saucepan, melt remaining butter and add flour, stirring constantly. Add 1 cup half-and-half, and cook on medium for 5 minutes. Cut cheese into small pieces and add to pot. Cook on medium, stirring frequently, until cheese is melted. Add half-and-half as needed to keep sauce from becoming too thick.

Add cheese sauce to crawfish-mushroom sauce. Combine well. Add cooked pasta and mix well. Serves 6.

Crawfish Jambalaya

1½ sticks butter
2 medium onions, diced
1 small bell pepper, diced
2 stalks celery, diced
1 can Ro-tel diced tomatoes
2 tsp. minced garlic
1½ tsp. salt
½ tsp. black pepper
¼ tsp. cayenne pepper
1½ cups chopped mushrooms
1 lb. peeled crawfish tails
2-3 cups cooked rice

Melt butter over medium heat. Add onions, bell pepper, and celery. Cook for approximately 30-40 minutes, stirring frequently. The vegetables should be very tender and slightly brown. Add Ro-tel, garlic, and seasonings; mix well and cook for 5 minutes. Add mushrooms and crawfish, cover, and cook for 5 minutes. Uncover and cook for 5 minutes more. Remove from heat and mix in cooked rice to desired consistency. Serves 6-8.

Crabmeat au Gratin

1 stick butter
1 medium onion, diced
2 tsp. salt
1 tsp. cayenne pepper
5 tbsp. flour
2 cups half-and-half
1$^1/_2$ cups whole milk
1 cup shredded cheddar cheese
2 egg yolks
2 lb. jumbo lump crabmeat, picked for shells
1 cup shredded cheddar cheese, for topping

In a medium saucepot, melt butter over medium heat. Add onion; sauté for about 10 minutes. Add seasonings, then flour, while stirring constantly. Add half-and-half and milk, and bring to a boil. Stir in 1 cup cheese. When the cheese has melted, remove from heat. Add egg yolks; mix well. Fold in crabmeat. Put in buttered gratin dishes. Top each with cheese. Bake gratins at 400 degrees for about 15 minutes, or until cheese is melted and bubbly. Serves 8.

Mulate's Crabmeat Stuffing

2 sticks margarine
3 medium onions, diced
2 medium bell peppers, diced
2 stalks celery, diced
1 tbsp. minced garlic
1 tbsp. Mulate's Cajun Seasoning, or salt and pepper to taste
12 hamburger buns
1 bunch green onions, chopped
2 tbsp. chopped parsley
3 eggs
1 lb. claw crabmeat, picked for shells

Melt margarine and cook onions, bell peppers, celery, and garlic over medium heat until tender and caramelized, about 45 minutes. Add Cajun seasoning and mix well. Set aside.

For these next steps, it's best to use your hands. In a large bowl, crumble hamburger buns. Add green onions and parsley, and mix well. Add eggs, and blend well. Add vegetable seasoning from above, and mix well. Fold in crabmeat. Makes approximately 2 lb. stuffing. Use this delicious stuffing to make one of our great dishes—Stuffed Mushrooms, Catfish Cecilia, Stuffed Bell Peppers, and Stuffed Crabs (see index).

Seafood Casserole

1 stick butter
1 cup diced onion
1 cup diced bell pepper
1 cup diced celery
2 cloves garlic, chopped
$1/4$ tsp. salt
$1/2$ tsp. cayenne pepper
$1/2$ tsp. black pepper
1 can cream of mushroom soup
1 can cheddar cheese soup
$1/3$ cup chopped parsley
1 cup chopped green onions
1 lb. uncooked shrimp
1 lb. claw crabmeat
1 lb. crawfish tails (optional)
2 cups cooked white rice
Breadcrumbs

Preheat oven to 350 degrees. In a large saucepot, melt butter. Add onion, bell pepper, celery, and garlic and cook until tender. Add dry seasonings and mix well. Add soups, parsley, green onions, and seafood. Cook until heated thoroughly, about 15 minutes. Stir in rice and $1/4$ cup breadcrumbs. Put into a 3-qt. casserole, and sprinkle top with more breadcrumbs. Bake for 30-45 minutes. Serves 6-8.

Joyce Boutté Kolb
Arnaudville, LA

Mirliton Dressing

4 large mirlitons
1 lb. shrimp, peeled and deveined
$^{1}/_{2}$ stick margarine
1 tbsp. salt
1 tsp. black pepper
$^{1}/_{4}$ tsp. cayenne pepper
$^{1}/_{2}$ tsp. dried sweet basil
$^{1}/_{2}$ tsp. onion powder
$^{1}/_{2}$ tsp. garlic powder
$^{1}/_{2}$ lb. white crabmeat, picked for shells
1 cup breadcrumbs
$^{1}/_{2}$ cup grated Parmesan cheese
3 tbsp. sweet butter

Preheat oven to 375 degrees. In a large stockpot, boil mirlitons in water until fork tender. Cut them in half, peel, remove the large seed, and coarsely chop the flesh. In a large nonstick pan, sauté mirlitons and shrimp in margarine for about 3 minutes. Add dry seasonings and cook for about 3 more minutes; remove from heat. Add crabmeat and $^{1}/_{2}$ cup breadcrumbs—mix well. Place mirliton dressing in a 9x13 baking dish. Sprinkle remaining breadcrumbs and Parmesan cheese on top—dot with butter. Bake for 40-45 minutes. This dressing is delicious as a main course or side dish.

Variation: You can use crawfish tails in place of the shrimp—add them when you add the crabmeat since they are precooked.

Tiffa Boutté
New Orleans, LA

Stuffed Bell Peppers

4 medium bell peppers
Mulate's Crabmeat Stuffing (see index)

Cut peppers in half and remove seeds. Blanch bell peppers by placing them in boiling water for about 5 minutes. Stuff with crabmeat stuffing.

To bake, place stuffed bell peppers on a baking sheet. Bake at 350 degrees for 20-25 minutes.

Fried Stuffed Bell Peppers

2 eggs, beaten
1 cup milk
3 cups breadcrumbs
3 cups oil for frying

Combine eggs and milk. Dip stuffed bell peppers into egg wash and then coat with breadcrumbs. Fry at approximately 350 degrees until golden brown. Serve with Tartar Sauce (see index).

Stuffed Crabs

8 crab shells, cleaned well
Mulate's Crabmeat Stuffing (see index)

Stuff shells with crabmeat stuffing.

To bake, place stuffed crabs on a baking sheet. Bake at 350 degrees for 20-25 minutes.

Fried Stuffed Crabs

2 eggs, beaten
1 cup milk
3 cups breadcrumbs
3 cups oil for frying

Combine eggs and milk. Dip stuffed crabs into egg wash and then coat with breadcrumbs. Fry at approximately 350 degrees until golden brown. Serve with Tartar Sauce (see index).

Fried Oysters

3 cups cornmeal
2-3 tsp. salt
1 tsp. cayenne pepper
32 fresh oysters
2-3 cups oil for frying

Place cornmeal in a 9x13 pan. Add salt and cayenne to your taste, and mix well. Put oysters in seasoned cornmeal, 8-10 at a time. Coat oysters well. Fry in oil at 375 degrees for 4-5 minutes. Serve with Cocktail Sauce (see index). Serves 4.

Catfish Cecilia

8-10 catfish filets, 7-9 oz. each
2 tsp. salt
2 tsp. cayenne pepper
Mulate's Crabmeat Stuffing (see index)
Flour for dusting filets
$\frac{1}{4}$ cup oil

Season filets with salt and cayenne. Cut a slit in the thick part of the cat-fish on the top side of the filet. Stuff opening with the Crabmeat Stuffing. Lightly dust the stuffed side of the filet with flour. Heat oil in pan. Place filets in pan, flour side down. Cook over medium-high heat for about 8 minutes. Flip filets and cook for 5-7 minutes more. Serves 8-10.

Fried Catfish

8-12 catfish filets, 2-3 oz. each
3 cups cornmeal
2-3 tsp. salt
1 tsp. cayenne pepper
2-3 cups oil for frying

Rinse and dry catfish. Place cornmeal in a 9x13 pan. Season cornmeal with salt and cayenne to your taste, mixing well. Put catfish filets in seasoned cornmeal, two or three at a time. Coat filets well. Fry in oil at 375 degrees for 6-7 minutes. Serve with Tartar Sauce (see index). Serves 4.

Catfish Mulate's

4 catfish filets, 7-9 oz. each
1 tsp. salt
1 tsp. cayenne pepper
¼ cup oil
Flour for dusting filets
Crawfish Etouffée (see index)

Season filets with salt and cayenne. Heat oil in a large pan over medium-high heat. Lightly dust one side of the filets with flour. Place filets in pan flour side down. Cook catfish about 7 minutes, then flip over. Cook for about 5 minutes more. Place catfish filets on plates and top with Crawfish Etouffée. Serves 4. This is our specialty of the house.

Cabbage Rolls

1 lb. ground beef
1 lb. ground pork
1 medium onion, diced
1 medium bell pepper, diced
2 cloves garlic, chopped
1 cup uncooked rice
1 egg
1 8-oz. can tomato sauce
1 tsp. salt
1 tsp. cayenne pepper
1 tsp. black pepper
1 large head cabbage
1 15-oz. can tomato sauce
$^1/_4$ cup light-brown sugar

In a large bowl, combine meat, onion, bell pepper, garlic, rice, egg, small can tomato sauce, and seasonings. Core cabbage and place head in boiling water. Pull leaves off as they begin to wilt slightly. Place equal parts of meat mixture in center of cabbage leaves. For each leaf, fold ends, roll up, and close with a toothpick. Place rolls in a roasting pan. Mix the large can tomato sauce with brown sugar and pour over rolls. Cover and bake at 350 degrees, basting occasionally, for 1 1/2 hours. Makes about 10-12 cabbage rolls. Serves 5-6.

Joyce Boutté Kolb
Arnaudville, LA

Hamburger Steak Lafayette

2$\frac{1}{2}$ lb. ground beef
2 eggs
1 small onion, diced
$\frac{1}{2}$ small bell pepper, diced
2 cloves garlic, minced
1 tbsp. Mulate's Cajun Seasoning
2 tbsp. Worcestershire sauce
$\frac{1}{2}$ cup breadcrumbs
4 slices American cheese

In a large bowl, mix all ingredients (except cheese) using your hands—it's a little messy but the easiest way to do it. Once you've mixed it thoroughly, form 4 large, flat patties. Cook patties to your liking in a large nonstick skillet over medium heat. Place cheese slices over patties right after you remove them from the heat.

Mushroom-Onion Gravy

1 tbsp. oil
1 small onion, diced
3 cloves garlic, minced
$\frac{1}{2}$ cup sliced mushrooms
1 can golden mushroom soup
1 can beef broth
$\frac{1}{2}$ cup water
$\frac{1}{2}$ tsp. cayenne pepper

In a medium saucepot, heat oil over medium heat and add onion and garlic. Sauté for about 10 minutes, until onions are tender. Add mushrooms, then golden mushroom soup and mix well. Add beef broth and water and stir until all ingredients are combined. Let the gravy simmer over medium to medium-high heat for about 15 minutes. Add cayenne and remove from heat. Smother your hamburger steaks in this delicious gravy! Serves 4.

Spaghetti and Meat Sauce

2 medium onions, diced
5 cloves garlic, chopped
1 1/2 tbsp. extra-virgin olive oil
1 1/2 lb. ground chuck
1 can tomato paste
3 cans tomato sauce
3 cans water
1 tbsp. sugar
2 tsp. salt
1 tsp. black pepper
2 tsp. dried sweet basil
1 lb. spaghetti

In a large, heavy pot, over medium-high heat, sauté onions and garlic in olive oil until transparent, about 15-20 minutes. Add ground chuck and cook until the meat is no longer pink. Stir in tomato paste, and then pour in tomato sauce. Fill the empty tomato sauce cans with water and add to pot. Stir and add sugar, salt, and pepper. Bring to a boil, then reduce heat and simmer for 45 minutes, stirring every 10 minutes or so to prevent sticking. Add basil and continue simmering for another 45 minutes.

I like to let my sauce stand for about 1 hour (or more) before serving—to let all of the flavors come together. You know how sauce is always better the next day!

Boil spaghetti in salted water and drain. Add about 1/2 cup sauce to the spaghetti and stir. Serve sauce over spaghetti and top with a little Parmesan cheese, if desired. Serves 6-8.

Boutté Burgers

1 1/2 lb. ground chuck
Mulate's Cajun Seasoning
8 slices fresh white bread
Mustard
Mayonnaise
4 leaves iceberg lettuce, washed

Make 4 hamburger patties and sprinkle Cajun seasoning on each side. On a flat-top grill or in a nonstick sauté pan, cook patties to your liking over medium-high heat. A well-done patty will take about 4 minutes on one side, and then 2-3 minutes on the other side. Lightly coat 4 slices of bread with mustard. Coat the other 4 slices of bread with mayonnaise. Place patties and lettuce in each sandwich. Serves 4. These hamburgers are done in the simplest way—and they're delicious!

Kerry Boutté
Owner, Mulate's of New Orleans

Stuffed Brisket

1 large onion, minced
1 medium bell pepper, minced
4 cloves garlic, minced
1 1/2 tsp. salt
1 1/2 tsp. cayenne pepper
5 lb. brisket

Preheat oven to 300 degrees. Mix vegetables and dry seasonings. Cut small holes in the brisket and fill with seasoning mixture. Bake covered for 3 hours. I like to slice the brisket with an electric knife to get really thin slices of meat. Serves 6-8.

Mulate's Chicken and Sausage Jambalaya

2 tbsp. Mulate's Cajun Seasoning
1 lb. boneless, skinless chicken thighs
1 lb. boneless, skinless chicken breasts
1 tbsp. oil
2 sticks margarine
2 cups water
4 medium onions, diced
1 medium bell pepper, diced
3 cloves garlic, chopped
1 lb. smoked sausage, cut into $1/2$-inch pieces
1 pt. fresh mushrooms, sliced
1 can Ro-tel diced tomatoes
4 cups cooked rice

Season all chicken pieces. In a large pot, heat oil and brown chicken. Remove chicken from pot and cut into bite-size pieces. Add margarine, $1/2$ cup water, and onions to pot. Cook onions over medium-high heat until dark golden brown, about 30-40 minutes. Add water as needed for sticking. Add bell pepper and garlic. Continue cooking and stirring frequently for 15 minutes. Add chicken, sausage, mushrooms, and Ro-tel tomatoes, and any remaining water to pot. Reduce heat to medium low and continue cooking for 45 minutes, stirring occasionally. Mix with cooked rice. Serves 8.

Pork Chop Jambalaya

8 pork chops, each $^1/_2$ inch thick
1 tbsp. Mulate's Cajun Seasoning
2 tbsp. peanut oil
1 large onion, diced
1 small bell pepper, diced
2 cups uncooked rice
1 tsp. salt
1 tsp. black pepper
$^1/_4$ tsp. cayenne pepper
4 cups water or chicken broth

Season pork chops with Cajun seasoning. In a Dutch oven, heat oil and brown pork chops. When chops are browned, remove them from the pot. Add onion and bell pepper; and cook until golden brown. Add rice and sauté for about 2-3 minutes. Add dry seasonings and water, and mix well. Place pork chops on top, and bring to a boil. Turn heat to low and cook until rice is done. Serves 4.

Tiffa Boutté
New Orleans, LA

Pork Chop Etouffée

4 center-cut pork chops, bone in
1-2 tbsp. Mulate's Cajun Seasoning
1 tbsp. oil
2 medium onions, diced
1 medium bell pepper, diced
2 cups water
2 cups cooked white rice

Trim excess fat from pork chops. Lightly coat each side with Cajun seasoning. In a large pan, heat oil over medium to medium-high heat and
brown pork chops. You want the pork chops to stick slightly to the pan.
After chops have browned nicely on each side (10-15 minutes total), take
them out of the pan. Put onions and bell pepper into pan. Add water and
stir—scraping all of the browned "debris" from the bottom of the pan.
Place pork chops back into pan and simmer partially covered for 45 minutes. Remove cover and simmer for 10-15 minutes more. Serve over rice.
Serves 4.

Stuffed Pork Roast

1 large onion, minced
1 medium bell pepper, minced
3 cloves garlic, minced
1$\frac{1}{2}$ tsp. salt
1$\frac{1}{2}$ tsp. cayenne pepper
5 lb. pork roast (a rump roast works well for this recipe)
1-2 tbsp. Mulate's Cajun Seasoning

Preheat oven to 300 degrees. In a medium bowl, combine onion, bell pepper, and garlic. Add salt and cayenne, and mix well. Cut 6 to 8 1-inch slits in the meaty areas of the roast—approximately 1-2 inches deep. Stuff these holes with the onion seasoning mix. Season outside of roast with Cajun seasoning. Place roast in pan and bake covered for 3-4 hours. Using a fork, check roast for tenderness—try to see how well the meat separates. When you cook a pork roast on a low temperature for a long time, the roast becomes very tender (and delicious). If the meat separates easily, the roast is cooked to perfection.

Red Beans and Rice

1 lb. smoked sausage, cut into ¹/₂-inch pieces
1 large onion, diced
1 small bell pepper, diced
1 large clove garlic, chopped
1 stalk celery, diced
1 lb. red beans, rinsed
10 cups water
1¹/₂ tsp. salt
1 tsp. cayenne pepper
4 cups cooked white rice

In a large pot, brown sausage over medium-high heat, remove from pot, and set aside to drain. Add onion, bell pepper, garlic, and celery to pot. Reduce heat to medium and cook until onions start to caramelize. Add beans, water, salt, and cayenne. Boil gently, uncovered over medium heat, stirring occasionally for about 1¹/₂ to 2 hours. Add more water if necessary. Add browned sausage and heat through. Serve over rice. Serves 6-8.

Kay Boutté
New Orleans, LA

Sausage and Tomato Gravy

1 lb. sausage, cut into bite-size pieces
1 medium onion, diced
1 medium bell pepper, diced
2 stalks celery, diced
8-oz. can tomato sauce
14.5-oz. can whole tomatoes
1 can Ro-tel diced tomatoes
3 oz. tomato paste ($^1/_2$ small can)
1 cup water
2 cups cooked white rice

In a large saucepot, brown sausage over medium heat. When thoroughly browned, remove from pot. Add onion, bell pepper, and celery—sauté for 5 minutes. Add sausage back to pot and cook for 3 minutes. Add tomato sauce, whole tomatoes, Ro-tel tomatoes, and tomato paste, and mix well. Add water and mix well. Bring mixture to a simmer, cover partially, and cook over medium to low heat for 45 minutes, stirring occasionally. Serve over rice. Serves 4.

Kay Boutté
New Orleans, LA

Side Dishes

Serving lunch

Had a two steppin' good time!
WYOMING, RHODE ISLAND

You are the greatest!
OPELOUSAS, LOUISIANA

Those green beans are excellent!
BATON ROUGE, LOUISIANA

Loved the green beans!
MANCHESTER, CONNECTICUT

Had the Sweet-Potato Crunch at a private party—absolutely delicious!
CHICAGO, ILLINOIS

Baked Beans

4 cans pork and beans
$^1/_2$ cup ketchup
$^1/_2$ cup brown sugar
1 tbsp. Worcestershire sauce
1 tbsp. lemon juice
1 tsp. yellow mustard
1 lb. bacon
1 medium onion, diced
$^1/_4$ cup water

In a large bowl, mix all ingredients together, except bacon, onion, and water.

Set aside 6-8 strips of bacon. Fry the rest of the bacon until crisp. Remove bacon from pan. Drain off most of the bacon grease, leaving just enough to coat the bottom of the pan. Add onion to the pan and cook over medium heat. When onion starts to wilt, crumble cooked bacon into the pan and mix well. Add water. Cook until onion is transparent. Remove from heat and add to the bean mixture.

Pour into a 9x13 baking pan. Place uncooked strips of bacon on top of beans. Cover with foil and bake for 1 hour at 375 degrees. After 1 hour, remove foil and bake uncovered for 30 minutes at 400 degrees. Serves 8-10.

Kay Boutté
New Orleans, LA

Green Bean Casserole

2 16-oz. cans French-cut green beans, drained
1 can cream of mushroom soup
3$^1/_2$-oz. can Durkee onion rings

Preheat oven to 350 degrees. Mix beans and soup in a large saucepot. Cook over medium heat just until warm. Place in a baking dish. Sprinkle onion rings on top and bake for 5-10 minutes, until browned.

Variation: You can add 1 cup shredded processed cheese to the green-bean mixture.

Sautéed Haricots Verts

$^3/_4$ stick butter
1 medium onion, diced
2 pkg. frozen green beans, thawed
1 tsp. cayenne pepper
1 tsp. black pepper

Melt butter, add onion, and cook on medium heat until tender. Add beans and seasonings. Cook for about 15 minutes. Serves 6.

Smothered Okra

1 tbsp. oil
1 medium onion, diced
1½ lb. cut okra (fresh or frozen)
1 can Ro-tel diced tomatoes
1 tsp. salt

In a medium saucepot, heat oil. Add onion and cook over medium heat for about 8 minutes. The onions should be just turning transparent. Add okra and continue to cook over medium heat. The okra will be slimy. Cook until the slime disappears—12-15 minutes. Add tomatoes and salt. Cook over low heat for another 20-25 minutes. Serves 4-6.

Smothered Cabbage

1 lb. smoked sausage, cut into bite-size pieces
1 large onion, diced
1 medium head cabbage, chopped
1 tsp. salt
¼ tsp. cayenne pepper
½ tsp. black pepper

In a large saucepot, brown sausage over medium heat. Add onion and sauté for 3 minutes. Add cabbage and cover. Cabbage will wilt as it cooks. Cook for about 50 minutes, or until cabbage is tender, stirring occasionally. Uncover, add seasonings, and cook for 5 minutes more. Serve as a side dish or as a main dish over rice.

Kay Boutté
New Orleans, LA

Cabbage Casserole

1 medium head cabbage
1 can cream of mushroom soup
$^2/_3$ cup milk, or half-and-half
$^1/_2$ lb. grated cheddar cheese

Quarter cabbage, and boil until tender. Drain thoroughly. Place cabbage in 9x13 baking pan. In a small bowl, mix soup and milk together. Pour over cabbage. Top with cheese. Bake at 400 degrees for 30-45 minutes. Casserole should be bubbling and cheese should be melted.

Kay Boutté
New Orleans, LA

Cauliflower with Cheese Sauce

1 medium head cauliflower
2 tbsp. butter
2 tbsp. flour
$^1/_4$ tsp. salt
$^1/_4$ tsp. cayenne pepper
1 cup milk
1 cup shredded processed cheese
5 drops hot sauce

Cut cauliflower into florets. Cook by placing in boiling water, stems down, and covering. Boil gently for 20 minutes, or until tender. Drain and place in a serving dish.

In a medium saucepot, melt butter over medium-high heat. Add flour and seasonings, and mix well with a whisk. Add milk and bring to a boil. Boil for 1 minute, then remove from heat. Add cheese and hot sauce, and mix until a well-blended sauce is created. Pour sauce over cauliflower and serve.

Kay Boutté
New Orleans, LA

Kerry watches as Tiffa prepares the corn for the macque choux

Corn Macque Choux

9 ears corn
$1/4$ cup oil
1 onion, chopped
$1/2$ small bell pepper, chopped
1 tsp. salt
$1/2$ tsp. black pepper
$1/4$ tsp. cayenne pepper

Using a knife, cut the corn off the cobs. Using the blunt edge of the knife, scrape the cobs to get all of the juices. Heat oil in large saucepot. Add corn and juices and cook on medium heat for 10 minutes. Add remaining ingredients. Cook for 40 minutes, stirring frequently. Serves 6-8.

Tiffa Boutté
New Orleans, LA

Cornbread Dressing

4 pkg. cornbread mix, plus ingredients to prepare
1 can cream-style corn
1 lb. ground beef
2 containers dressing mix*
1¹/₂-2 qt. low-sodium chicken broth
2 tbsp. butter

Make cornbread according to package directions, adding corn before baking. Bake and set aside.

Brown beef and add dressing mix. Cook partially covered over medium heat, stirring frequently, for 10 minutes. Remove from heat. Crumble cornbread into large mixing bowl. Add meat mixture. Mix well, using the chicken broth to provide moisture to the dressing. Pour into two 9x13 baking pans. Dot the tops with butter. Bake at 350 degrees for 50 minutes. This is a perfect dish for the holidays!

*Dressing mix is a vegetable, meat, and seasoning mixture that is usually used to make rice dressing. It can be found in the frozen section of your grocer's meat department. If it is unavailable, use 2 lb. ground pork in its place, and sauté 1 diced onion and 1 diced bell pepper in 1 tbsp. oil before browning the pork. You will also need to add about 1 tbsp. salt, 2 tsp. black pepper, and 1 tsp. cayenne pepper to the meat mixture.

Mary and Gab Robin
Port Barre, LA

Rice Dressing

1 tbsp. oil
1 medium onion, diced
1 medium bell pepper, diced
1 lb. ground beef
1 lb. ground pork
2 tsp. salt
1$\frac{1}{2}$ tsp. cayenne pepper
$\frac{1}{2}$ tsp. black pepper
1 tsp. garlic powder
1 cup chopped green onions
3 cups cooked white rice

In a large saucepot, heat oil over medium heat. Add onion and bell pepper.
Cook for about 10 minutes, stirring frequently. Add beef and pork, and
brown for about 15 minutes. Add dry seasonings and continue to simmer
for about 10 minutes more. Turn the heat off and remove most of the excess
grease. Add green onions and stir. Add rice and mix until well blended.
Serves 8. This is a quick and easy recipe!

Spaghetti and Cheese

16 oz. thin spaghetti
14 slices American cheese
1 stick butter
1 egg, beaten
1 cup whole milk
1 tsp. cayenne pepper

Cook and drain spaghetti. Break 8 cheese slices into pieces. In a large bowl,
mix hot spaghetti, cheese pieces, and butter. When butter and cheese have
melted, add the egg, milk, and cayenne. Put into greased 9x13 glass dish.
Place the 6 whole cheese slices on top of the spaghetti mixture. Cook at 350
degrees for 25 minutes. Serves 8-10.* This dish is great for the holidays!

*You can cut this recipe in half. However, you should still use 1 egg.

Creamed Spinach

1 stick butter
1 tsp. flour
1 pkg. frozen chopped spinach
$\frac{1}{2}$ cup milk
$\frac{1}{2}$ cup heavy cream
$\frac{1}{4}$ tsp. salt
$\frac{1}{2}$ tsp. cayenne pepper

In a medium saucepot, melt butter over medium heat. Add flour and mix well. Add spinach, milk, cream, and seasonings—mix well. Simmer over medium heat for 10 minutes. Serves 4.

Eggplant Casserole

1 large eggplant
1 lb. sausage meat or ground beef
1 stick butter
2 medium onions, diced
1 small bell pepper, diced
3 stalks celery, diced
1 tbsp. minced garlic
1 cup chicken broth
1 tsp. salt
1 tsp. cayenne pepper
2 cups breadcrumbs
2 eggs, beaten

Peel eggplant and cut into small pieces. Cook in boiling salted water (about 1 tsp. salt) until tender. Drain and set aside. Brown meat, drain, and set aside. In a large saucepot, melt butter over medium heat. Add onions, bell pepper, celery, and garlic and sauté until tender, about 20 minutes. Add chicken broth, salt, and cayenne and cook for 5 minutes more. Add eggplant and meat, mix well, and remove from heat. Add breadcrumbs, 1 cup at a time, mixing well. Add eggs, mixing until well blended. Pour dressing into a 9x13 baking pan. Bake at 350 degrees for 25 minutes. Serves 10-12.

Everyday Potatoes

2 links smoked sausage
2 large onions, diced
3 lb. red potatoes
1/4 cup oil
1 tsp. salt
1 tsp. cayenne pepper

Slice sausage into 1/4-inch slices. Brown the sausage over medium heat.
Add onions and cook until onions start to wilt. Remove sausage and
onions from pot and set aside. Peel potatoes and cut into bite-size pieces.
Add oil to the pot. Once oil is hot, add potatoes and brown over medium
heat. Cook uncovered and stir from bottom every 2-3 minutes to prevent
sticking. You may need to add water to help prevent sticking. When potatoes start to get tender, add sausage and onions back to pot. Add seasonings. Cook until potatoes are completely cooked and tender.

Mark Robin
Port Barre, LA

Mashed Potatoes

6 medium red potatoes (about 2 lb.)
3/4 stick butter
2/3 cup milk, or half-and-half
1 tsp. salt
1/2 tsp. black pepper

Peel potatoes. Cut potatoes into 1-2-inch pieces. Boil until tender.
Remove from pot and drain. Place butter in the same pot and add drained
potatoes. Smash potatoes, and incorporate butter. Add milk and seasonings, blending well. I like to use a hand mixer to get smooth and creamy
mashed potatoes. Adjust seasonings to taste. Serves 4-6.

Stuffed Potatoes

4 strips bacon
2 large baking potatoes
$^1/_2$ stick butter
$1^1/_4$ cups shredded cheddar cheese
$^1/_4$ cup chopped green onions
$^1/_2$ cup sour cream
$^1/_2$ tsp. salt
$^1/_4$ tsp. cayenne pepper

Preheat oven to 400 degrees. Fry bacon until crispy and crumble. Rinse and dry potatoes. Wrap potatoes individually in aluminum foil. Bake for 1 hour 15 minutes. Remove from oven, unwrap, and slice in half lengthwise. While keeping the skin in tact, scoop potato out of the skin and put flesh into a medium-sized bowl. Add butter and mix well. Add all other ingredients (except 1 cup cheese) and mix until well blended. Put potato mixture back into skins. Sprinkle cheese over the potatoes. Bake at 350 degrees for 15 minutes, or until cheese has melted. Serves 4.

Sweet-Potato Crunch

2 30-oz. cans sweet potatoes, drained, or 4 lb. boiled, skinned
    sweet potatoes
1¼ cups sugar
1 tsp. salt
1 tsp. cinnamon
4 eggs
1 cup half-and-half, or heavy cream
1 tsp. vanilla
1 stick butter, melted

Preheat oven to 350 degrees. Mash sweet potatoes, then add all ingredients and mix well. Pour into greased 9x13 baking dish.

Topping

1 box light brown sugar
$^2/_3$ cup flour
$^2/_3$ stick butter, melted
2 cups chopped pecans

Mix brown sugar and flour. Add butter and pecans. Mix well until fully incorporated. Spread on top of sweet-potato mixture, and bake for 35 minutes. Serves 12. This is a great holiday dish!

Desserts

The BEST Bread Pudding!
BLOOMINGTON, ILLINOIS

Great food—Bread Pudding is the best I've ever had!
MINNEAPOLIS, MINNESOTA

Best Bread Pudding ever!
GRANITE FALLS, NORTH CAROLINA

Excellent Bread Pudding—I love it!
LAFAYETTE, LOUISIANA

The best food & entertainment of our whole vacation (which included a cruise!!)
VICTORIA, BRITISH COLUMBIA, CANADA

Banana Nut Bread

1 stick butter, softened
1 cup sugar
2 eggs, beaten
4 medium bananas, mashed
1$\frac{1}{2}$ cups flour
1 tsp. baking soda
$\frac{1}{2}$ cup chopped pecans

Preheat oven to 350 degrees. Cream butter and sugar. Add eggs and bananas and mix well. Add flour, baking soda, and pecans; mix well. Bake for 40-50 minutes in a 9x5 loaf pan. Or divide mixture in half and bake for 30-40 minutes in two 8x3 loaf pans.

Kay Boutté
New Orleans, LA

Banana Pudding

2 boxes banana pudding, 3 oz. each
$\frac{1}{2}$ box vanilla wafers
3 medium bananas, cut into $\frac{1}{2}$-inch pieces

Prepare pudding according to box instructions. Cover the bottom of a casserole dish with a layer of wafers and a layer of bananas. Pour $\frac{1}{3}$ of pudding over first layer. Continue to layer wafers, bananas, and pudding to make 3 layers of each. The top layer will be pudding. Place wafers around the outer edge of the dish as a garnish.

Monique looks on as Kerry prepares Bananas Foster

Bananas Foster

4 bananas
1 1/2 sticks butter
3/4 cup brown sugar
2 cinnamon sticks, or 1 tsp. ground cinnamon
1/2 cup banana liqueur
1/2 cup rum
Vanilla ice cream

Delicious Bananas Foster

Cut the bananas, crosswise at a slant, into 2-inch pieces. Melt butter in large saucepan. Add brown sugar and cinnamon, and stir constantly for about 1 minute. Add bananas and banana liqueur, and cook bananas for about 30 seconds on each side. The mixture should be simmering. Add rum, remove from heat, and immediately light with a match. Shake pan until flame goes out, and then serve over ice cream. Serves 6-8.

Kerry Boutté
Owner, Mulate's of New Orleans

Chocolate Praline Sheet Cake

2 cups sifted flour
2 cups sugar
2 sticks butter
1 cup water
4 tbsp. cocoa powder
1 tsp. vanilla
1 tsp. baking soda
$^1/_2$ cup half-and-half
2 eggs, beaten

Preheat oven to 350 degrees. Mix flour and sugar. In a small saucepot, bring butter, water, and cocoa to a boil and pour into flour mixture. Add vanilla, soda, and half-and-half—mix well. Add eggs and mix well. Pour into nonstick 9x13 baking pan. Bake for 45 minutes.

Chocolate Pecan Fudge Icing

$^3/_4$ stick butter
3 tbsp. cocoa powder
$^1/_4$ cup half-and-half
$^3/_4$ box confectioners' sugar
1 cup pecans

In a medium saucepot, over medium-high heat, melt butter. Add cocoa and half-and-half. Cook for 5 minutes. Remove from heat, and add confectioners' sugar and pecans—mix well. Spread over cake while both are still hot.

Dirt Cake

8-oz. pkg. cream cheese
6-oz. pkg. cream cheese
$1/2$ cup melted butter
$1/2$ cup confectioners' sugar
$2^2/3$ cups cold milk
1 large box vanilla instant pudding
12 oz. Cool Whip
4 cups Oreo cookie crumbs

In a large bowl, beat cream cheese, butter, and sugar until smooth. Alternate adding milk and pudding mix and incorporate well into mixture, beating about 2 minutes. Add Cool Whip and beat until thoroughly mixed. Layer in glass bowl starting with Oreo crumbs on the bottom, and ending with Oreo crumbs on the top.

The Best Fig Cake Ever

$1/2$ cup sugar
3 eggs
1 cup oil
8 oz. sour cream
2 cups flour
2 tsp. cinnamon
1 tsp. salt
1 tsp. baking soda
1 cup chopped pecans
$1^1/2$ cups fig preserves with syrup

Preheat oven to 350 degrees. Cream sugar and eggs. Add oil and stir. Add sour cream and mix well. In a separate bowl, combine flour, cinnamon, salt, and soda. Add dry mixture to wet mixture. Stir in pecans and figs. Pour into baking pan or Bundt pan and bake for about 50 minutes or until a toothpick inserted in cake comes out clean. Fresh whipped cream or Cool Whip makes a great topping.

Goldie Comeaux
Owner, Mulate's of Breaux Bridge

Coconut Sour Cream Layer Cake

1 box yellow butter cake mix, plus ingredients to prepare
2 cups sugar
16 oz. sour cream
12 oz. fresh-frozen coconut, thawed
1¹/₂ cups heavy cream

Prepare and bake cake mix according to instructions on box using two 8-inch round cake pans. After cake has cooled, split layers with thread—this will give you 4 layers.

Mix sugar, sour cream, and coconut. Blend well and chill. Set aside 1 cup mixture and keep chilled. Spread the remaining filling between the layers of cake.

To prepare the icing, combine the remaining filling with heavy cream. Beat on medium speed until thick and smooth. Spread on top and sides of cake. Place cake in an airtight container and refrigerate for 2-3 days before serving. I always ask my mom to bake this cake for special occasions—it's so delicious!

Tip: Place a glass bowl and the beaters in the freezer to chill before preparing the icing.

Kay Boutté
New Orleans, LA

Homemade White Butter Cake

1$^1/_2$ sticks sweet butter, softened
1$^1/_2$ cups sugar
2 cups flour
2 tsp. baking powder
$^1/_4$ tsp. salt
$^3/_4$ cup egg whites (approximately 6 egg whites)
$^3/_4$ cup milk
3 tsp. vanilla

Preheat oven to 350 degrees. Grease the bottom of two 9-inch round pans or one 9x13 pan. Line the bottom of the pan with wax paper.

In a large bowl, cream butter and sugar until light and fluffy. In a separate bowl, mix together flour, baking powder, and salt. In a separate bowl, mix egg whites, milk, and vanilla. Add flour mixture and milk mixture alternately to the butter mixture, starting and ending with flour mixture. Make sure to scrape the bowl and beater.

Pour batter into prepared pan(s). Bake for 30 minutes, or until a toothpick inserted into the center comes out clean. Cool in pan for 5 minutes, then turn out, remove wax paper, and cool completely. Delicious with Pecan Cake Filling (see index).

Hawaiian Pineapple Cake

2 cups buttermilk biscuit mix
1 cup flour, sifted
1 tsp. baking soda
³/₄ cup sour cream
1 stick margarine
1 cup sugar
2 tsp. vanilla
3 eggs
20-oz. can crushed pineapple, juice reserved
2 tbsp. rum

Combine mix, flour, and baking soda. In another bowl, beat sour cream, margarine, sugar, and vanilla for 2 minutes. Add eggs and beat for 1 minute longer. Add dry mixture and beat for another minute. Add drained pineapple and rum, and blend well. Pour into greased Bundt pan. Bake at 350 degrees for 45 minutes.

Glaze

³/₄ cup sugar
¹/₄ cup reserved pineapple juice
¹/₄ cup margarine
2 tbsp. rum

In a small saucepot, combine sugar, juice, and margarine and stir over low heat until sugar is dissolved. Remove from heat and add rum. Pour half of glaze over cake right when it's removed from the oven. Wait 10 minutes, then turn the cake onto a serving plate and pour over remaining glaze.

Ida Colon Boutté
Arnaudville, LA

Piña Colada Cake

1 box yellow butter cake mix, plus ingredients to prepare
20-oz. can crushed pineapple
1 cup sugar, divided
$1/3$ cup Coco Lopez Cream of Coconut
3 tbsp. Captain Morgan's Spiced or Coconut Rum
1 box vanilla instant pudding, plus ingredients to prepare
1 cup heavy cream
1 cup flaked sweetened coconut, toasted

Prepare and bake cake mix according to instructions on box. Meanwhile, combine the pineapple, $3/4$ cup sugar, and cream of coconut in a small saucepan and bring to a boil over medium heat, stirring constantly to prevent sticking. Reduce heat to medium low and simmer for about 15 minutes. Remove from heat, add rum, and set aside.

When cake has finished baking, remove from oven and, using a fork, pierce holes throughout the cake. Pour hot pineapple mixture over cake and set aside.

Prepare pudding as directed. Spread pudding over hot cake and pineapple mixture. Refrigerate until cooled completely.

Whip cream with remaining sugar until soft peaks form. Cover top of cake with whipped cream and sprinkle with toasted coconut.

Cover and refrigerate overnight.

Strawberry Shortcake

2 lb. fresh strawberries, halved
$^1/_4$ cup + 1 tbsp. sugar
12 tbsp. Grand Marnier
$1^1/_2$ cups strawberry jam
1 lb. mascarpone cheese
1 cup heavy cream
1 tsp. vanilla
2 pound cakes (12 oz. each), cut into $^1/_2$-inch slices

Place the halved strawberries in a bowl. Sprinkle 1 tbsp. sugar over the berries. Stir in 4 tbsp. Grand Marnier. Place bowl in refrigerator and let "marinate" for 6 hours.

Stir the strawberry jam and 4 tbsp. Grand Marnier in a small bowl to blend.

Using an electric mixer, blend the mascarpone cheese and remaining Grand Marnier in a large bowl. Again, using an electric mixer, beat the cream, remaining sugar, and vanilla in another large bowl until soft peaks form. Stir about $^1/_4$ of the whipped cream into the mascarpone cheese mixture, and then fold in the remaining whipped cream.

Line the bottom of a 9x13 glass dish with one of the sliced pound cakes. Spread half of the jam mixture over the cake slices. Spread half of the mascarpone cheese mixture over the jam mixture. Layer half of the strawberries over the mascarpone cheese mixture. Repeat the layers starting with the sliced pound cake and finishing with the other half of the strawberries.

Cover and refrigerate overnight. The mascarpone cheese gives this classic an Italian twist!

Sock It to Me Cake

$^1/_2$ cup + 1 tbsp. sugar
1 stick margarine
4 eggs
$^1/_2$ pt. sour cream
1 box yellow butter cake mix, sifted
3 tbsp. chopped pecans
3 tbsp. light brown sugar
1 tbsp. cocoa powder

Cream $^1/_2$ cup sugar and the margarine. Add eggs one at a time, mixing well. Add sour cream—use hand mixer to blend well. Add cake mix—blend well and beat for 4 minutes with hand mixer. In a separate bowl, combine pecans, brown sugar, cocoa, and 1 tbsp. sugar to make a filling. Pour half of cake batter into greased Bundt pan. Sprinkle filling in as next layer. Pour rest of batter in. Bake at 350 degrees for 45 minutes.

Frosting
1 cup confectioners' sugar, sifted
2 tbsp. melted butter
2 tbsp. hot milk
1 tsp. vanilla

Combine all ingredients, and mix well. Pour over the cake while still warm.

Ida Colon Boutté
Arnaudville, LA

Fruit Delight

15-oz. can pitted black cherries
11-oz. can mandarin orange slices
20-oz. can pineapple chunks
1 tbsp. confectioners' sugar
1 pt. sour cream
1 bag mini marshmallows

Drain fruit, mix together, and sprinkle with confectioners' sugar. Stir in sour cream and marshmallows.

Lemon Ice Box Pie

2 cups finely crumbled vanilla wafers
$1/2$ cup melted butter

Mix ingredients. Line a pie pan with this mixture. Chill for 30 minutes before adding filling.

Filling

3 egg yolks
1 can condensed milk
$1/2$ cup fresh-squeezed lemon juice
1 tsp. finely grated lemon zest

Preheat oven to 300 degrees. Beat egg yolks until light and fluffy. Add condensed milk and mix well. Slowly add lemon juice (the juice "cooks" the eggs and thickens the mixture). Stir in lemon zest. Pour into prepared crust. Bake for 30 minutes. Top with whipped cream if desired.

Pecan Pie

1 cup white corn syrup
$^1/_2$ cup light brown sugar
3 eggs
1 tsp. vanilla
Pinch salt
1 cup pecan halves
1 unbaked pie shell

Preheat oven to 350 degrees. Mix all filling ingredients together. Pour into pie shell. Bake for 50 minutes.

Variation: You can add $^3/_4$ cup semisweet morsels for Chocolate Pecan Pie.

Milk Chocolate Peanut Butter Crunch Fudge

3 cups sugar
$^2/_3$ cup evaporated milk
$1^1/_2$ sticks butter
11.5-oz. bag milk chocolate chips
7 oz. marshmallow creme
3 tbsp. crunchy peanut butter

Bring sugar, milk, and butter to a rolling boil. Let the mixture boil for 5-6 minutes. Remove from heat, and stir in chocolate chips until melted. Add marshmallow creme and peanut butter and stir until well blended. Pour into nonstick 9x13 pan and let cool before cutting into squares.

Pralines

2 cups sugar
1 cup light brown sugar
$\frac{1}{4}$ tsp. salt
$\frac{1}{2}$ cup condensed milk
$\frac{1}{4}$ cup butter
$\frac{1}{2}$ cup whole milk
3 cups pecan halves

Combine all ingredients except pecans in a large saucepan. Bring mixture to a boil slowly over medium heat, stirring frequently. Boil until soft ball forms when a little bit of the mixture is dropped into water. Add pecans. Remove from heat, and stir for 3-5 minutes or until creamy. Drop by spoonfuls onto wax paper. Let cool for 30 minutes. Makes 12 large or 24 small pralines. These are delicious by themselves, or you can crumble 1 praline on top of 2 scoops vanilla ice cream for a wonderful dessert!

Mulate's Homemade Bread Pudding

6 eggs
1 tsp. vanilla
2 cups whole milk
2 cups half-and-half
1 cup sugar
6 hamburger buns
$\frac{1}{2}$ cup raisins

Preheat oven to 350 degrees. In a large bowl, whip eggs, and then add vanilla, milk, and half-and-half. Mix well. Add sugar, and mix well. Grease a 9x13 pan. Break hamburger buns into pieces and place in greased pan. Sprinkle raisins evenly throughout the bun pieces. Pour egg mixture over buns. Using your fingers, make sure that all bun pieces are soaked with the mixture. Bake for approximately 45 minutes. If you prefer a firmer texture, chill for about 2 hours, then reheat for serving.

Butter Rum Sauce

$\frac{1}{2}$ stick butter
$\frac{1}{4}$ cup sugar
$\frac{1}{2}$ cup half-and-half (or heavy cream)
$\frac{1}{2}$ cup rum

Melt butter. Add sugar and cook on medium heat for 3 minutes. Add half-and-half and rum and cook for 5 more minutes or until slightly thickened. Serve warm over bread pudding. Serves 8-10. This dish is a customer favorite!

Pineapple-Coconut Bread Pudding

6 eggs
6 oz. Coco Lopez Cream of Coconut
2 cups half-and-half
$1^1/_2$ cups whole milk
1 cup sugar
8-oz. can crushed pineapple, juice reserved
6 hamburger buns
$^1/_2$ cup toasted coconut

Preheat oven to 350 degrees. In a large bowl, whip eggs, and add cream of coconut, half-and-half, and milk. Mix well. Add sugar and pineapple, and mix well. Grease a 9x13 pan. Break hamburger buns into pieces and place in pan. Sprinkle toasted coconut evenly throughout the bun pieces. Pour mixture over buns. Using your fingers, make sure that all bun pieces are soaked with the mixture. Bake for approximately 45 minutes.

Tropical Rum Sauce

4 oz. Coco Lopez Cream of Coconut
Reserved pineapple juice
$^1/_4$ cup sugar
$^1/_2$ cup half-and-half, or heavy cream
$^1/_2$ cup coconut rum*

In a small saucepan, simmer cream of coconut and pineapple juice on medium heat. Add sugar and cook for 3 more minutes. Add half-and-half and rum and cook for 5 more minutes or until slightly thickened. Serve over warm bread pudding.

*If coconut rum isn't available, use regular rum in its place.

No-Bake Chocolate Sweets

2 cups sugar
$^1/_2$ tsp. white corn syrup
2 sticks butter
$^1/_2$ cup milk
4 tbsp. cocoa powder
1 cup peanut butter
1 tsp. vanilla
3 cups uncooked quick oats

Bring sugar, corn syrup, butter, milk, and cocoa to a rolling boil, and then remove from heat. Add remaining ingredients, and mix well. Drop by tablespoons onto wax paper. Makes 40 candies.

Kay Boutté
New Orleans, LA

Peach Cobbler

2 large cans peaches, 29 oz. each
1 stick butter
2 cups sugar
2 cups self-rising flour, sifted
$^1/_2$ cup half-and-half
1 cup milk

Drain peaches. Melt butter in a 9x13 baking pan. In a medium bowl, mix sugar and flour. Add half-and-half and milk, and mix until well blended. Pour batter over melted butter. Place peaches on top of batter. Do not stir. Bake at 350 degrees for 1 hour.

Kay Boutté
New Orleans, LA

No-Bake Delight

³/₄ cup graham-cracker crumbs
³/₄ cup finely chopped pecans
¹/₄ cup sugar
¹/₃ cup melted butter
8 oz. cream cheese, softened
¹/₄ cup sugar
2 tbsp. milk
12 oz. Cool Whip
1 large box chocolate instant pudding
2²/₃ cups cold milk
Grated chocolate or chopped pecans for garnish

Combine crumbs, pecans, sugar, and butter. Press into bottom of a 9x13 glass dish. Beat cream cheese, sugar, and 2 tbsp. milk until smooth. Fold in half of the Cool Whip. Spread over crust. Prepare pudding as directed on box, using milk. Pour over cream-cheese layer. Spread remaining Cool Whip over pudding. Sprinkle grated chocolate or chopped pecans on top. Chill 2-3 hours before serving.

Goldie Comeaux
Owner, Mulate's of Breaux Bridge

Peanut-Butter Chocolate-Chip Cookies

2 cups peanut butter, creamy or crunchy
2 cups sugar
2 eggs, beaten
¹/₂ cup milk chocolate chips

Preheat oven to 350 degrees. Mix ingredients and drop by spoonfuls onto a nonstick cookie sheet. Flatten the cookies by making a crisscross pattern with a fork. Cook for 10-12 minutes. Makes approximately 30 cookies.

Sand Tarts

1 cup butter, softened
$^1/_2$ cup confectioners' sugar
$^1/_2$ tsp. vanilla
$1^3/_4$ cups sifted all-purpose flour
$^1/_2$ cup finely chopped nuts (pecans or almonds are best)
Confectioners' sugar for dusting

Preheat oven to 350 degrees. Cream butter and confectioners' sugar. Work in vanilla, flour, and nuts. Shape into small balls, logs, or crescents. Bake on ungreased cookie sheet for 20 minutes. Roll in powdered sugar when cool. These are great cookies for the holidays!

Pecan Mini Muffins

1 cup brown sugar
1 cup chopped pecans
$^1/_2$ cup flour
2 eggs, beaten
1 stick butter, melted

Preheat oven to 350 degrees. Mix brown sugar, pecans, and flour. Add eggs and butter and mix well. Spoon by tablespoons into mini muffin tins lined with mini muffin papers. Bake for 15-18 minutes. Makes 24 mini muffins.

Rich and Creamy Cheesecake

1 pkg. vanilla wafers, crushed
1 stick butter, melted

Combine ingredients. Press into bottom of spring-form pan.

Filling

24 oz. cream cheese
$^3/_4$ cup sugar
Juice of 1 large lemon
3 large eggs

Using a mixer, combine cream cheese, sugar, and lemon juice—blend well. Add eggs and mix until well blended and smooth. Pour into crust, and bake for 30 minutes at 350 degrees. Remove from oven, and let cool for 45 minutes.

Topping

3 cups sour cream
$^3/_4$ cup sugar
2 tsp. vanilla

Mix ingredients and pour over cooled cake. Return to 350-degree oven for 30 minutes. Remove from oven, cool to room temperature, refrigerate, and chill thoroughly.

Lagniappe

Monique and Kerry chop vegetables

Great Food, Good Music, thanks!
MILTON KEYNES, ENGLAND

Great food and entertainment!
BASTROP, LOUISIANA

Our first meal in New Orleans and it was fabulous!
BROOKLYN, NEW YORK

The best food I've ever had! Thank you!
MONTEREY PARK, CALIFORNIA

Great food & service!
TRINITY, ALABAMA

Pain Perdu

2 eggs, well beaten
1/2 cup sugar
1 tsp. vanilla
2/3 cup milk
2 tbsp. oil
6 slices white bread
Confectioners' sugar

In a shallow bowl, mix eggs, sugar, vanilla, and milk (in that order) until well blended. Heat oil over medium heat in a large pan. Dip bread into mixture, coating well on both sides. Allow excess to drip off, and place in pan. Brown on both sides, remove, and drain on paper towels. Sprinkle with confectioners' sugar. Serve with syrup, if desired. If you like, you can add a little cinnamon or nutmeg when the sugar is added. This dish is also known as "lost bread" or French toast.

Couche-Couche

1/4 cup oil
2 cups cornmeal
1 tsp. baking powder
1 1/2 tsp. salt
3/4 cup milk
3/4 cup water

Heat oil in heavy pot. Mix dry ingredients. Add milk and water (batter will be soft). Pour batter into hot oil; allow crust to form before stirring. Crust will stick to the bottom of the pan. Reduce heat to low and stir occasionally until cooked, about 15 minutes. Serve with milk and sugar as a cereal.

Banana Pancakes

2 cups buttermilk biscuit mix, sifted
1 tbsp. sugar
2 tsp. baking powder
1 cup milk
2 tbsp. lemon juice
2 eggs, well beaten
2 ripe, medium bananas

Mix dry ingredients together. Add milk, lemon juice, and eggs. Mix until well blended. In a small bowl, mash bananas then add to batter—mix well. Cook on hot griddle (or nonstick pan) until top bubbles, then flip over and cook until golden brown. Makes 8-12 pancakes.

Kay Boutté
New Orleans, LA

Cajun-Style Party Mix

1¹/₂ sticks margarine
3¹/₂ tbsp. Worcestershire sauce
2 tsp. hot sauce
3 tsp. Mulate's Cajun Seasoning
¹/₂ tsp. garlic powder
¹/₂ tsp. onion powder
3 cups each Corn Chex, Rice Chex, and Wheat Chex
2 cups mixed nuts
2 cups bite-size cheese crackers
1 cup bite-size pretzels

Heat oven to 250 degrees. In a large roasting pan, melt margarine in oven. When melted, remove pan and stir in sauces and seasonings. Add dry ingredients and mix until coated well. Roast for 1 hour, stirring every 15 minutes. Makes 14 cups.

Chili Cheese Dip

1 lb. lean ground beef
1 can Ro-tel diced tomatoes
1 tsp. cumin
1 tsp. onion powder
$^1/_2$ tsp. garlic powder
24 oz. processed cheese

Brown meat over medium-high heat, and drain excess grease. Reduce heat to medium, and add tomatoes and seasonings. Cook for 5 minutes. Add cheese and cook, stirring frequently, until cheese is melted. Serve with tortilla or corn chips.

Taco Dip

1 lb. ground beef
1 pkg. taco seasoning
1 can refried beans
1 pt. sour cream
8 oz. salsa, or picante sauce
2 cups shredded cheddar cheese
Black olive slices
Jalapeño slices
Tortilla or corn chips

Brown beef and drain. Prepare with taco seasoning according to package instructions. Set aside to cool for 20 minutes. Using a 9x13 dish, layer the ingredients in the following order: beans, beef, sour cream, salsa, cheese, olives, jalapeño. Serve with chips. This easy dip is always a favorite at our Louisiana State University football parties!

Variation: If you would like to add guacamole, layer it after the sour cream.

Kerry and Tiffa's Ciabatta-Lotta

1 loaf Ciabatta bread
1 tbsp. olive oil
¼ lb. sliced smoked ham
¼ lb. sliced salami
¼ lb. sliced mortadella
¼ lb. sliced cappicola
8 slices provolone cheese
Olive Salad (see index)

Slice the Ciabatta in half horizontally and drizzle olive oil on both pieces of bread. Layer the meats and cheese on the bottom slice of the bread. Spread a generous portion of Olive Salad all over the top layer of cheese. Place the top half of the bread back on the bottom to form a large sandwich. Cut into 4 pieces and serve. This is Kerry and Tiffa's version of a New Orleans favorite—the muffaletta!

Kerry and Tiffa Boutté
New Orleans, LA

Cocktail Sauce

2 cups ketchup
1 tbsp. prepared horseradish
2 tsp. hot sauce

Mix all ingredients. Serve with Boiled Shrimp, Fried Catfish, or Fried Oysters (see index).

Tartar Sauce

2 cups mayonnaise
3 tbsp. sweet relish
1 tbsp. diced onion

Mix all ingredients. Serve as a dipping sauce with fried seafood or Stuffed Crabs (see index).

Homemade Cornbread

1¼ cups cornmeal
¾ cup boiling water
1 tsp. salt
2 tsp. sugar
3 tsp. baking powder
2 tbsp. melted butter
¼ cup all-purpose flour
½ cup evaporated milk
¼ cup water
1 egg, beaten

Preheat oven to 400 degrees. Put cornmeal in medium mixing bowl, pour boiling water over cornmeal, and mix well. Set aside to cool. In another mixing bowl, combine remaining ingredients and blend well. Add cornmeal mixture to other mixture, and blend well. Let the mixture sit for 10-20 minutes. Pour into nonstick square baking pan. Bake for 30 minutes. This cornbread is really good for breakfast the next day. Put one square in a bowl and heat in the microwave for about 40 seconds. Sprinkle with sugar and pour in about ½ cup milk. Eat it like cereal—it's delicious!

Cracklin' Cornbread

1 1/4 cups cornmeal
3/4 cup boiling water
1 tsp. salt
1 1/2 tsp. sugar
3 tsp. baking soda
1 tbsp. butter
1/4 cup all-purpose flour
1/4 water
1 egg, well beaten
8 oz. pork cracklin', coarsely chopped

Preheat oven to 400 degrees. Place cornmeal in a bowl and add boiling water. Mix well and set aside to cool. Meanwhile, in a large mixing bowl, combine all remaining ingredients except the cracklin'. Add cooled cornmeal mixture and mix until well blended. Fold in cracklin' and place mixture in a greased 9x9 pan. Bake for 20 minutes or until a toothpick inserted in the center comes out clean.

Tiffa Boutté
New Orleans, LA

Mexican Cornbread

2-3 pkg. cornbread mix (16-18 oz. total), plus ingredients
   to prepare
1 can cream-style corn
$1/2$ cup diced jalapeño pepper
$1^1/_2$ lb. ground beef
4 tbsp. chili powder
1 tsp. salt
8 slices American cheese

Preheat oven to 350 degrees. Prepare cornbread mix according to package instructions, but do not bake yet. Add corn and $1/4$ cup pepper, and mix well. Brown ground beef. Add chili powder, salt, and remaining pepper, and mix well. Cook for about 5 minutes. Pour half of the cornbread mixture into a 9x13 baking pan. Spread the chili mixture over the first layer of cornbread. Layer the cheese across the chili layer. Pour remaining cornbread mixture over the top of the cheese. Bake for 50-60 minutes or until golden brown.

Mary and Gab Robin
Port Barre, LA

Crawfish Mango Salsa

1 lb. crawfish tails, peeled
2 ripe mangoes, peeled and chopped
1-2 jalapeño peppers, seeded and diced
$^1/_2$ bunch cilantro, chopped
$^1/_2$ cup fresh-squeezed lime juice
2 tbsp. soy sauce
$^1/_2$ tsp. sesame oil
Endive leaves or tortilla chips

Rinse crawfish tails and coarsely chop. Combine crawfish with mangoes (reserve $^1/_2$ cup), peppers, and cilantro (reserve 3 tbsp.). Add lime juice, soy sauce, and sesame oil—mix well. Place in refrigerator for at least 3 hours. When ready to serve, add reserved mango and cilantro for bright color. Spoon onto endive leaves or serve with chips.

Tiffa Boutté
New Orleans, LA

Crawfish Quiche

1 cup shredded Swiss cheese
1 small onion, minced
1 lb. crawfish tails
2 frozen pie shells (9 inch)
4 large eggs
2 cups heavy cream
1 tsp. salt
$^1/_4$ tsp. cayenne pepper
$^1/_8$ tsp. sugar

Preheat oven to 400 degrees. Place half of the cheese, onion, and crawfish tails in each pie shell. In a mixing bowl, beat eggs, then add in the rest of the ingredients, mixing until well blended. Pour half of this mixture into each pie shell. Bake for 15 minutes. Reduce heat to 350 degrees and bake for 30-45 minutes more—until tops of quiches have browned slightly. Serve at room temperature. Serves 6-8.

Mary and Gab Robin
Port Barre, LA

Cheese Grits and Pork Chop Etouffée

5 cups water
$^3/_4$ tsp. salt
1 cup grits
3 tbsp. butter
1 cup shredded cheddar cheese
Pork Chop Etouffée (see index)

In a medium saucepot, boil water and salt. Add grits while stirring constantly. Reduce heat to medium low and cover pot. Cook for 15 minutes, stirring every 3 minutes or so. Remove from heat, add butter and cheese, and mix until both are melted. Serve with Pork Chop Etouffée. This dish (my version of grits and grillades) is perfect for brunch!

Olive Salad

1 cup pitted green olives
1 cup pitted black olives
1 cup pimento-stuffed green olives
1 large carrot, minced
1 stalk celery, thinly sliced
$^1/_2$ medium onion, diced
4 cloves garlic, minced
Olive oil

Put all vegetables into a glass jar and cover completely with oil. Close jar and shake well. Place jar in refrigerator for 1 week—shaking jar daily. Use Olive Salad as is, or run through a food processor. Serve atop greens in a salad or on a Ciabatta-Lotta (see index).

Tiffa Boutté
New Orleans, LA

Pecan Cake Filling

1 stick butter
1 cup sugar
1 cup evaporated milk
2 cups pecan meal*

In a medium saucepot, melt butter. Add sugar and milk. Simmer for 4 minutes, until thick, and then remove from heat. Add pecan meal, and mix well. You can use this between the layers and on the outside of a cake. I like this filling with the Homemade White Butter Cake (see index).

*Pecan meal is like cornmeal—finely ground pecans. You can make it in a food processor.

Variation: Add 2 tbsp. cocoa powder when adding sugar and milk.

Remoulade Dressing

2 cups mayonnaise
$^{1}/_{2}$ cup + 1 tbsp. Creole mustard
2 tsp. Worcestershire sauce
6 dashes hot sauce
$^{1}/_{2}$ tsp. paprika

Mix all ingredients. Serve as a dipping sauce with grilled or fried alligator. You can add shrimp, crabmeat, or crawfish to the dressing and serve as a salad on top of chopped lettuce. This is also Mulate's house dressing—delicious on salads of any kind!

Tiffa's Seasoning Blend

1 cup salt
1 cup garlic powder
1 cup onion powder
$^{1}/_{2}$ cup dried oregano leaves
$^{1}/_{2}$ cup dried sweet basil
$^{1}/_{4}$ cup dried thyme leaves
$^{1}/_{4}$ cup black pepper
$^{1}/_{4}$ cup cayenne pepper
$1^{1}/_{4}$ cups sweet paprika

Combine all ingredients in a food processor and pulse until blended well. Use as a general cooking seasoning.

Tiffa Boutté
New Orleans, LA

Cocktails

Wonderful! Great food, music & dance! Fun for all!
RICHMOND, VIRGINIA

Only place we eat when we come! Always delicious!
KATY, TEXAS

Great time—good people.
KENT, WASHINGTON

Always enjoyable—this was our 3rd visit in the past week! Awesome!!
LODI, WISCONSIN

Excellent all around—my feet are still tappin'!
SANTA ROSA, CALIFORNIA

Cajun Bloody Mary

1 shot pepper vodka
1 shot beef broth
Dash Worcestershire sauce
$\frac{1}{2}$ tsp. horseradish
Dash salt
Dash black pepper
Dash celery salt
Tomato juice
Olives
Pickled green beans

Fill a 12-oz. glass with ice. Add vodka and beef broth. In a separate small container, mix Worcestershire sauce and horseradish, then add to glass. Add dry seasonings, and fill with tomato juice. Mix well. Serve with olives and pickled green beans.

Hurricane

$\frac{1}{2}$ shot 151 rum
$\frac{1}{2}$ shot rum
Splash melon liqueur
Orange juice
Hurricane mix

Fill a 12-oz. glass with ice. Add both rums and melon liqueur. Fill with orange juice and Hurricane mix.

Louisiana Lemonade

1 shot lemon rum
Splash grenadine
Splash sour mix
Lemonade
Cherries for garnish

Fill a 12-oz. glass with ice. Add rum, grenadine, and sour mix. Fill with lemonade, and mix. Garnish with cherries.

Mint Julep

Mint leaves
Simple syrup
1 shot bourbon

Muddle mint with a splash of simple syrup in the bottom of an 8-oz. glass. Add lots of ice. Add bourbon. Fill with simple syrup.

Plantation Tea

$\frac{1}{2}$ shot lemon rum
$\frac{1}{2}$ shot orange vodka
Splash melon liqueur
Splash sour mix
Cola
Ginger ale

Fill a 12-oz. glass with ice. Add rum, vodka, melon liqueur, and sour mix. Fill with cola and ginger ale. Mix well.

Twisted Cosmo

1 shot orange vodka
Splash lime juice
6 oz. cranberry juice
$\frac{1}{2}$ shot Cointreau
Lime twist

Fill a martini shaker with ice. Add the liquids and shake for 20 seconds. Strain into a martini glass. Garnish with lime twist.

Zydeco Tornado

1 shot melon liqueur
Splash pineapple juice
Splash orange juice
1 shot rum
1 shot spiced rum
Splash cranberry juice
Orange slice
Cherry

Fill glass with ice. Layer ingredients in order, starting with the melon liqueur on the bottom. When layering the juices, move your hand in a circular motion around the top of the glass—this helps to achieve the beautiful layered look of the drink. Garnish with an orange slice and a cherry.

Index